Soft Blows the Wind

Mary of Walsingham

Mary of Walsingham
White Rose of England,
Jewel of the ages past,
Awesome prophetess
listen To me, broken,
Lifeless, torn apart.
Meet me in the Slipper Chapel,
Take me to your heart

Holy mile lead me home,
Willow trees
beside the river,
Where the shadows
break and quiver,
Take me to the little chapel
Where we fell in love.

Grey stone walls
Of ruined Priory,
Ancient days
of gothic archways,
Point me to the little chapel
Where I live again.

Fr Jimmy Collins

Soft Blows the Wind

(On Foot to Walsingham)

Fr Jimmy Collins

GRACEWING

First published in 2003

Gracewing
2 Southern Avenue, Leominster
Herefordshire HR6 0QF

ISBN 0 85244 569 5

Typesetting by Action Publishing Technology Ltd,
Gloucester, GL1 5SR

Printed in England by
Antony Rowe Ltd, Eastbourne BN23 6QT

Contents

Part I - The Story of a Pilgrimage

Introduction   vii
          Our Lady of Walsingham   x
Chapter 1. How it Started   3
         2. Upholland to Horwich. Rain and mud.   7
         3. Path Finding   11
         4. Harden Moor   14
         5. Rochdale and the Pennine Way   18
         6. The Pennine Way   25
         7. Over Soldier's Lump and the Laddow
             Rocks   29
         8. The Dark Peak   34
         9. Derbyshire   40
        10. Tragedy   44
        11. Trial and Pilgrimage   50
        12. Between Derby and Nottingham   55
        13. Middle England   63
        14. Still Middle England   68
        15. Waltham on the Wolds   74
        16. Waltham to the Blue Cow   77
        17. Stella and John   83
        18. Day of Rest   88
        19. The Fen Country   92
        20. The Road to King's Lynn   96
        21. King's Lynn   102
        22. Norfolk   106
        23. Walsingham   111

Part II – The Pilgrimage Route

A Pilgrimage			117
Useful Information			119
Information Centres			120
Suggested accommodation en route			122
Hostels and Youth Centres			125
Catholic Churches			127
Itinerary:	Horrock Hall to Adlington	Map 1	129
	Adlington to Belmont	Map 2	132
	Dimple to Ramsbottom	Map 3	136
	Ramsbottom to Whitworth	Map 4	140
	Whitworth to Whitehouse Pub	Map 5	143

The Pennine Way

	Whitehouse Pub to Marsden	Map 6	146
	Marsden to Crowden	Map 7	149
	Crowden to the Snake Pass	Map 8	152
	The Snake Pass to Edale	Map 9	154

The Limestone Way

	Edale to Millers Dale	Map 10	156
	Millers Dale to Monyash	Map 11	159
	Monyash to Youlgreave for Bonsall	Map 12	162
	Bonsall, Cromford & the Midshires Way	Map 13	165

The Midshires Way

	Midshires Way to Duffield	Map 14	168
	Duffield to Dale Abbey	Map 15	171
	Dale Abbey to Kegworth	Map 16	174
	Kegworth to Bunny	Map 17	176
	Bunny to Upper Broughton	Map 18	179

The Mowbray Way

	Upper Broughton to Chadwell	Map 19	181
	Chadwell to Buckminster	Map 20	184

The Viking Way

	Buckminster to South Witham on to Castle Bytham	Map 21	186
	Castle Bytham to Witham-on-the-Hill	Map 22	189

The Macmillan Way

Thurlby and through the Fens	Map 23	191
Though the Fens to Spalding	Map 24	193
Spalding to Holbeach	Map 25	195
Holbeach to Little London	Map 26	197
Little London to Terrington St Clement	Map 27	199
Terrington St Clement to King's Lynn	Map 28	201
King's Lynn to Congham	Map 29	203

The Peddars Way

Congham to Great Bircham	Map 30	205
Great Bircham to South Creake	Map 31	208
South Creake to Walsingham	Map 32	210

Introduction

This book was never meant to be published. The pilgrimage arose out of deep desire in my heart to thank the Mother of Jesus for the part she had played in moulding my life as a priest. When I finished the pilgrimage I was living at Upholland College, surrounded by the unique beauty of that incomparable place, filled as it was with the atmosphere of years of prayer and scholarship. I sat down and typed what was in my heart as I walked the road and pathways that led me to the Slipper Chapel.

I tossed it aside when it was written, but subsequently someone asked if they could read it. It was then passed from hand to hand, and the demand to print it became clamorous. I decided that I would seek to do that. Maps of the journey were drawn up covering the walk: one series by a young cartographer whose name was Jane and finally one by Tony Turner (this was the one accepted). The manuscript was re-typed by Mr John Leicester, who also sent me some financial help towards this book in memory of his devoted wife who had recently died, and finally Tony took the whole matter up and painstakingly over a long winter and spring talked the reluctant author into action.

This is the result, and I make no apologies for it because it was a task of real love.

It is interesting that, since the original pilgrimage was made, the new Footpath Laws have resulted in an opening-up of the countryside, and a major pathway known as the Midshires Way has linked the Pennine Way to the South of England as far as the Causeway. The Macmillan Way from the

South Coast also links in at the end of the journey. Hence the material is valid for a large number of pilgrims from both north and south.

My prayer is that many will follow where this has begun. May the people who walk to Walsingham have the same vision of Heaven that was granted to me.

Jimmy Collins 2002

Our Lady of Walsingham

The apparition of Our Lady in this spot was early in the eleventh century. So the first millennium had just ended and a new millennium was under way. It was not a good time in England. The great king Alfred had beaten back the Danish Vikings, and his sons had followed him on the throne of England. But you must not think of England as it is today.

Offa's Dyke on the Welsh borders and the remains of Hadrian's Wall across the north remind us that the Welsh, the Scots, and the Vikings safely ensconced in Dublin, were always threatening. There was not really a unified country. Barons and Earls tended to fight among themselves and the loyalty of fighting men was loyalty not to a king or country but to the lord, the earl or the baron whose land they rented, not with money, but with a tenth part of the produce of their fields.

As far as I know, there was no clear picture of the state of the Faith in England at this time. No statistics: that would be a very late science. The first real look at the state of things was the Anglo-Saxon Chronicle. Later there was the Domesday book under William I, but that was some seventy years on. But a cultured guess would be that the parishes were staffed by priests who were very poorly educated. And remember there were less than two million people in England. There are now more people in London than in the whole of the country in the year 1000.

Although, as I say, there were few diocesan priests, there were many monks, and the monasteries supplied Mass and the sacraments to outlying villages which had sprung up and taken the shape that our present villages still have. The people had built a church. There were houses built around, made of wood and wattle (mud, cow dung and straw) and roofs made of thatch. Celibacy was not universal among the priests. In the Cathedral in Winchester at the time of Canute all the canons were married: Emma who ran the country gave them their marching orders, and the monks from a nearby monastery moved in.

Women were strong and important in Anglo-Saxon England. The men ploughed, cultivated the land and the forest, and hunted. The women made cloth, cooked, bore children, and sewed. Although, 'to the laity were recommended the duty of daily prayer, frequency of communion, the observance of festivals and fasts, the payment of church dues, the sanctity of marriage, and the abhorrence of pagan ceremonies (Dooms of Canute; Lingard. *History of the Anglo Saxon Church*), it seems nevertheless that the influence of the Christian Church was not strong enough to change old customs. The most recent research seems to indicate that an Anglo-Saxon wedding was more a case of a village festival than a church ceremony; and that made it possible for a woman to leave the 'partner' if the marriage did not succeed. Custom gave her certain rights over shared property and the care of the children.

One Anglo-Saxon law code makes it clear that a woman could walk away from her marriage if she wanted to, and if she took the children and cared for them, she was entitled to half the property. There was no Canon Law regulating marriage at this time.

It was into this half-settled world that Our Lady appeared at Walsingham, and requested that a house be built: a relic of the house at Nazareth where Mary and Joseph lived with the child Jesus. It was pointing out three important truths:

1. The importance of a settled family life.
2. That the Presence of Jesus in the home was central.
3. Here the people of England would find Faith and healing.

So it was done and the pilgrimages began and a new dawn of Faith came. It is notable that the reign of St Edward coincided with this, as some people say that Our Lady appeared at Lourdes in answer to the prayers of the Curé of Ars.

The Augustinian Friars built a graceful monastic church and a monastery, the ruins of which remain to this day. And for four hundred years the people of England and many from Europe came to pray at the sacred shrine.

The Black Death took its toll of the monasteries. The number of vocations declined. There were certain laxities in the Priory of Walsingham. A Visitation of the Bishop in the early sixteenth century (1515) found that there was only a small number of monks and lay brothers. They accused the Abbot and two other monks of drinking late into the night at the Bull, said the Abbot was too friendly with a lady, and that he personally owned two thousand sheep and had a larger income than the abbey itself. That was the accusation. We do not know whether it was true or not. In the closure of the major monasteries in the mid 1530s, Walsingham went with the rest. The statue of Our Lady was burnt in Smithfield, and the land and treasures of the Abbey were distributed to the friends of Thomas Cromwell and Latimer. It was the beginning of the decline into Protestantism.

You understand that this was more than an act of vandalism, It was a kind of blasphemy, The hatred was greater than explicable by normal means. There was something evil about it. Centuries passed. Then came the Anglican vicar Alfred Hope Patten, the buying of the Slipper Chapel, and the gradual restoration of the shrine. But underneath it all was the need for something deeper. It was as if a man or woman had been abused in childhood. It was evil. The memory tries to close it down. But always something remains. In order to set the being free, something had to be done to make reparation. It came in an extraordinary way at the end of the Second World War.

It was the period when many of the soldiers were demobbed after years of war and prison camps. They flooded back to a new Britain, purified by the austerity and poverty of wartime conditions.

An ex-officer named Osborne went on pilgrimage to Vezelay in France, where a great national meeting saluted the cross of Christ in thanksgiving for the freedom of France. He came back to England determined to do the same here. In the year 1948 he organized a cross-bearing pilgrimage from all parts of Britain. Fourteen crosses were carried by men from all corners of the country. They met in Walsingham and set up the crosses in the grounds of the Priory, and Mass was celebrated in the presence of some five thousand people. It was the answer to the Reformation. It closed the book. I knew some of the men. I was there and saw their feet as they walked down the Holy Mile, in total silence, carrying the crosses, and the Holy Mile was lined with people from all over the land. That day they purified the temple. That day opened a new era for the people of this land, and Mary entered into her own.

Part I

The Story of a Pilgrimage

Chapter 1

How it Started

Early in 1996 I decided that I would resign from my parish. The parish was St Joseph the Worker in the Archdiocese of Liverpool. It was situated in a town named Kirkby in the Metropolitan Borough of Knowsley. The town was a comparatively new one, created out of green fields at one time part of the estate of Lord Derby.

Farms had been worked on the estate from feudal times. But a long-standing slum problem in the city of Liverpool and widespread destruction by the Luftwaffe in World War II led the Liverpool City Fathers to purchase the land and begin the township of Kirkby to re-house the people. The new tenants were from an area of Liverpool which had been densely Catholic since the days of the Irish famine.

A multitude of churches had existed side by side in the inner city, along with schools and sodality halls, each parish with its ten thousand or so Catholics.

The discipline of the Church demanding that Catholics marry Catholics, and the dominance of a strong priest presence, had bred a ghetto mentality. But it was a very close community, with links between family and family, and links going back to grandparents. The Faith had been passed down and various customs and rituals, repeated year after year, bound together childhood, adolescence, married life and old age, up to the time when the coffin would stand on trestles underneath a window decorated with white curtains and flowers, and the families would come in to say the rosary before the Requiem.

But then they moved out . . . a biblical exodus to a promised land in new homes owned by a 'benevolent' Council; and,

3

within five years, sixty thousand people had settled in. Some thirty thousand were Catholics. Schools and churches were built.

The parishes were overshadowed by huge debts. During this time I had moved from a curacy at a seaside resort to a parish in Woolton on the outskirts of Liverpool. It was an exciting time. There was a lot of optimism in the air. People were becoming more prosperous. Full employment, the end of rationing, the music of the Beatles, the rise in the great Merseyside football clubs – it was a time of fast change. Men walked on the Moon; there were freedom marches, new ideas and a surge towards higher education by young people who had never had a chance previously.

I was very happy as a curate in a parish with a large Mass attendance, and a gentle and humble parish priest who was gifted with musical talent and a very keen intellect. He had served in the Navy in the First World War. For part of my time there I shared the company of two young priests, one at university and the other to be the first rector of a new teacher training college, Christ and Notre Dame. The insights of the Second Vatican Council were still being worked out. I became part of a catechetical team of school advisors, ran a big youth club, was chaplain to a big secondary modern school and a girls' grammar school; I visited home after home, using a bicycle to get around the parish, gave twice-weekly instruction to interested non-Catholics, many of whom entered the Church. I was very happy. Life was exciting, fulfilling, and I continually thanked God for choosing me to be a priest and using me. I did not want money. I had enough to live on. I did not really have any ambition to be a parish priest . . . in charge of things.

During this time my mother was moved into a nursing home in that very parish. She was in her seventies. My father had died some years before and I had been privileged to bless him and pray with him as he died. My mother was a very gentle Irishwoman; her only ambition had been to take care of her remaining three children. I had left home at eleven to be a priest, and when she died the world seemed empty. But I knew that she had gone to heaven, and tried to comfort my older sister Eileen and brother Kevin.

Some time after this I asked Archbishop Beck if I could go to work for some years in South America. I had bought tapes of a Spanish course on Linguaphone, and had done as much research as I could about the need for priests in South America. I had talked it over with Canon Murphy, the parish priest, and he had listened to me, as he always did: he was always so supportive of my wild ideas. Archbishop Beck also listened sympathetically. Two weeks later he sent for me, and asked me to become the parish priest of a new parish of St Joseph the Worker in Kirkby. The church and the house had been completed two years previously under the watchful eye of Fr John Smith who was suffering from stress and extreme exhaustion. I had bought a car from a worker at the new Ford factory at Halewood. I drove over to Kirkby and began a new life.

I was forty-eight years old. It was the beginning of Holy Week in a new area at its most turbulent time. The street were full of children 'playing out' and of teenagers at street corners, and big men who sometimes drank too much, and women who worked in factories and played bingo.

Thirty years later I left on the night of Easter Sunday. My life had changed, moulded, altered by the impact of those years and by the wisdom of the remarkable people who became my friends and helpers. I was conscious of this. The decision to leave had not been taken lightly. Many things had united to make it clear that it was time to go. The yearly round of first communion programmes had been broken by a diocesan decision to introduce new books which made impossible the Christine Brusselman programme we had followed with some success for eight years; the strain of marriage courses, confirmation courses, the feeling that things which I had embraced as challenges were now becoming too much; the death of Archbishop Worlock who had asked me to stay on after the age of seventy-five. All these things united to crystallize the need to make a decision that it was time to go. But the decision was being made over the months. From Christmas onwards I was also conscious of two other factors.

One ... that the priesthood had been the most wonderful gift that God had given me. The second, that under God, the next most wonderful gift had been the presence of the Blessed Virgin in so many of the events of my life. I wanted to thank her in some special way for her goodness to me.

So I determined that I would walk to Walsingham to thank her. I would walk all the way. I would go on my own; I would say Mass each morning. I would say the Joyful mysteries of the rosary on the road in the morning, the Sorrowful in the afternoon, the Glorious mysteries in the evening. I would meditate as I went on the wonders of the life of a priest. I would not be sponsored. I did not want publicity. It was to be a pilgrimage of thanksgiving. I told some of my friends. They were not happy about it. But I was determined. I was five foot two inches in height, I weighed nearly seven stone; and I was seventy-eight years old, and I knew I was right.

Chapter 2

Upholland to Horwich.
Rain and mud

The diocese had given me a room at Upholland College, where I had been educated for the priesthood. It was a beautiful room, overlooking the lake and the trees. My bedroom was adjacent, with a shower and some pieces of old furniture which I thought artistic. The Community College in Knowsley, of which I was still a governor, had given me a pair of boots ... 'Chris Brasher' fell-walking boots. Some of the parishioners at St Joseph's had bought a new rucksack for me. I had all I needed. On July 4th I rose at 5.30 a.m., said the first hours of the liturgical office of the day, celebrated Mass, had breakfast and packed the rucksack. By 7.15 a.m. I was on the road outside the College heading for a huge raking television mast on Winter Hill some twenty miles away, but clearly visible from the college. I had with me the Ordnance Survey maps needed, one and a quarter inches to the mile. The quiet by-roads, the footpaths, the hideous A roads, the monstrous motorways, they were faithfully reproduced on the maps. I had grown used to using a compass with the map and so felt fairly secure. Within fifteen minutes the rain came down, the skies were black as the peat on Soldier's Lump. I put on all my waterproofs, made for the paths clearly marked on the map through Dean Wood. Alas, the paths had been ploughed up! The wheat stood waist-high where the path ought to have been. The rain was pitiless. I slithered and slipped; the rucksack was heavy and swayed me alarmingly when I slipped. It took me an hour to negotiate the slopes of Dean

Wood. Time was going fast. My early start had been lost. The next stage was worse. I followed the footpath on the map and found myself in the wrong place: retraced my steps and tried again; followed a waymarked path and it led nowhere; just down a muddy slope to a stream.

I slithered down, crossed the stream. Climbing up the other side the weight of the rucksack and the insecure footing played havoc. I found myself on my back in the stream with cool water flowing gently over my face. I scrambled out. The waterproofs had kept me dry, the plastic bags wrapped around all clothing in the rucksack had saved them; only my boots were squelching. I left them like that, and regretted it later. I wandered through a jungle where there should have been a path. It was 10.15 a.m. I had been three hours on the journey and not gone a mile. Some two hundred and twenty miles lay ahead. I struggled through the undergrowth and found my way blocked by a thorn hedge and a high wooden fence. I was despairing by now and wondered if I had made a mistake. Maybe the Blessed Mother did not want me to do this after all.

I put my foot on a projecting plank of the fence and hauled myself up and saw right in front of my bewildered eyes a statue of St Bernadette, who saw the Blessed Virgin in Lourdes, and she seemed to be laughing at me. It lifted my heart. I dropped over the fence and saluted the little peasant girl. She was the first ray of light on a dark morning.

I sat down in the middle of Standish on a bench near a parish church. An old woman with shopping bags looked at me curiously, sitting there, the rain running off me and the boots caked with mud. But I felt happy. I was meant to be where I was. I began the first five decades of the rosary as I walked down a side road towards Adlington Lakes. The rain stopped, and I sat by the lakeside and ate some biscuits. The top of the flask had broken and it was not possible to drink the tea. I took off my boot and looked at the left foot; it was beginning to pain me. I put a pad of Dr Scholl's blister treatments on it, and changed the socks for dry ones. I found myself crossing a golf course, crossed a canal bridge and went into a pub for a pot of tea and a sandwich, and spent the afternoon trying to follow footpaths that weren't there and becoming more and more exhausted. But I was content. It was a pilgrimage. I said the Sorrowful mysteries of the rosary and felt I was one of them.

I reached Horwich at 7 p.m. I had already reconnoitred Horwich and knew that a pub called the Bull offered Bed and Breakfast. I had reckoned that Horwich had little to offer tourists and that I would certainly be able to find a vacancy in the Bull.

It was locked. I tried every door: there was no answer. I went to a police station which was right opposite, and made enquiries. The police officer on duty was helpful. 'It should be open,' he said. He phoned the Bull. Then he told me, 'They say they have no vacancies. They are already full.'

He advised trying a small hotel, just around the corner. I went in the direction indicated, but saw nothing that looked like a hotel. The evening was drawing in. Bolton was a few miles down the road. I thought, 'I'll get a bus to Bolton: there must be some place there.' I stood by a bus stop in Horwich. It was a long street, still wet from the rain. A few takeaway shops, a few lights beginning to appear in houses, but no one anywhere to be seen. It may have been Coronation Street time, but on that long street there was only me and a bus stop; both of us waiting for a bus that never came.

Suddenly out of the half-mist a child came riding a tiny bicycle. He must have been all of six years old. He stopped and looked at me. 'Where are you going?' said he, the way kids do. 'I'm going to Bolton,' I said.

'What for?' he asked. 'I'm looking for somewhere to sleep,' said I. 'Why don't you sleep here?' said the kid. 'There is nowhere open here,' I told him. The child stopped and seemed to ruminate. Then he looked at me. 'There is nowhere in Bolton,' he said. I said 'How do you know?' He said, 'I've been there; I didn't see anywhere to stay.' He rode off into the mist, and I thought, 'The child's right. I'll go and see the local priest.' It was about 8 p.m. The church was large and stood on a prominent position about half a mile down the road. The presbytery was adjacent, with a flight of stone steps leading up to it. I climbed the steps and rang the bell. No sign. I rang again and waited. Not even a dog barked. The house was silent.

I climbed down the steps, crossed the road and went into the pub. It was full of life. Behind the bar was a young man, podgy and friendly, and a barmaid who looked like him. I bought a Coke and explained my predicament. They were uncertain about B & Bs, so they called a conference of the beer drinkers standing around the bar. It was agreed by all that there were three possibilities. One was the small hotel mentioned by the policeman. The second was a pub called 'The Giggling Girls' . . . The what? I said. They explained that was not its real name, but it was the nickname given by the locals. The third suggestion was a hotel which they said could be expensive. I didn't think I could risk walking all those distances, so they rang for a taxi for me I mentally made notes. One . . . if you get stuck, don't go to a church: go to a pub! Two . . . taxi men are always helpful. The taxi drew up outside the small hotel. I got out and rang the doorbell. An Asian gentleman appeared. He looked at me. I knew then that I had lost a battle. 'There's no room here,' he said. His wife came down the stairs, took one look at me and re-affirmed: 'We're full up,' she said. I got back in the taxi and we drove to 'The Giggling Girls'. They were apologetic. We went to the 'expensive' hotel. This time the taxi driver took no chances. It was a private hire car, a Volvo. He was a very presentable young man. He got out of the taxi and rang the doorbell. 'I have a client who would like accommodation for one night,' he said. The proprietor said, 'Certainly, we have a single room vacant.' I stepped out of the car. His face dropped. But it was too late. I had made it!

Chapter 3

Path Finding

There were white clouds sailing in a blue sky when I set off the next morning. I had found new energy after the night's sleep and put fresh pads on the foot which had pained me so much yesterday. The tall mast on Winter Hill was on my left-hand side as I left Horwich by Walker Fold and went over the moorland. I was thinking about the episode yesterday when I got no answer at the church. It riled me: quite illogically it was stirring deep memories.

There was a time in the past years when every parish priest began locking their church. Well, not every parish priest. St Joseph the Worker had refused to be a locked church. During the thirty years of my ministry there, Kirkby was regarded as a high-risk area. There were times in the early years when this was true. In one period every telephone kiosk was vandalized and two of them were set alight just a few hundred yards down the road. Windows were smashed; every shop was clad nightly in enough chain mail to start a crusade; and some shopkeepers kept it on all day. The changing patterns of graffiti were more interesting than the gutter press, and most of the trees were uprooted in the park which bordered the presbytery. But every morning the church was open at 8 a.m. and did not close until 8.30 p.m. The men and women removed the altar cloths and the candles at the end of every Mass. The votive candles were put away; everything worth stealing was taken out of sight. The door of the church was open and people could go right up to the benches near the tabernacle or to the statues of St Joseph and the Immaculate Conception.

During those thirty years more than one person became a Catholic because they had found the church open and full of peace. In the midst of their mental and physical turmoil they had become aware of a mysterious and powerful presence when they sat down in an empty church where the red light of a sanctuary lamp bore witness to something they did not understand.

The children wandered in and asked questions about it. Teenagers came in, sometimes to find candles to light the 'rollies' with white powder in them. During the thirty years some things went missing and sometimes a door to the choir loft was jemmied. In the beginning windows were broken. We clothed them in plastic and stopped it. But they did not scrawl on the plaster on the walls. They did not write the things they wrote in bus shelters. In this socially turbulent area the children, the adolescents and the adults dealt honourably with a building they clearly regarded as sacred. It was interesting. Locked churches and locked presbyteries do not build Christian communities.

Locking churches was an arbitrary and paranoid action. It was the ultimate act of vandalism because it made it impossible for people to use it when they most needed it. There was a general sense of fear. The closure was not based on Faith or trust in God, or in the people. The trouble with it was that it had the permanency of a life sentence. The closed churches are now part of life and, sadly, part of the irrelevance of Christian Faith in a post-Christian world. The closed church was rapidly the closed presbytery

There used to be housekeepers; there were drawbacks in that system, but it was a human face at the door, a human voice on the telephone. Now they have been replaced by a microwave oven and an answerphone. Robots build cars, but microwaves and answerphones, locked churches and locked presbyteries do not build Christian communities.

We used to talk about this in St Joseph's when the supply of priests ran out, and the housekeeper left, so that I was alone in the house. The men and women agreed to man the door and the phone on a rotary system throughout the week. Most of them were unemployed, anyway, and they were delighted to have a job to fill in the time. They all used the kitchen to make tea. One room in the house was known as 'the clinic' because so many people came to pour out their troubles to whoever was on duty. A lot of them smoked and drank tea in 'the clinic' and many deep theological questions were raised and debated in a quite extraordinary way, as I can testify, having been there as an astonished and intrigued listener.

I learned as much as I taught, but no one was turned away from the door, everyone was welcomed, and when the phone rang a human voice answered. No one got paid, not even the priest: like some of them I was on a pension; the others were on the giro. But it worked.

I ruminated on this as I said the Joyful mysteries of the rosary that morning because somehow it fitted in with the theme. And at midday I sat in a field looking out over the moors towards Egerton in the sunlight. I took off my left boot and put on more Dr Scholl pads, drank tea from the flask and a plastic cup and smoked a café crème cigar. I lined up a footpath to Egerton on the map using the compass, followed the bearing because the path was non-existent on the ground, went steeply down a hill to a stream which I waded, and pulled myself up to the fourteenth tee of a golf course, to the surprise of the golfers.

Golfers are nice people; they told me how to escape from the golf course, and I walked down a deep valley into Egerton. It was 5 p.m. Time to find a Bed and Breakfast.

I wasted no time, went straight to the nearest pub, ordered a Coke, and put my case to the jury drinking pints of beer around the bar. They went into immediate action and 'phoned all available B & Bs in the locality. They were all fully occupied. Finally they found a single room for me at the Bull in Belmont.

Then one of the men (whom I had never met before) put down his half-finished pint and drove me to the Bull. I fell asleep thinking about Christian communities.

Chapter 4

Harden Moor

I woke early in the Bull and began the day's round. I celebrated Holy Mass in the bedroom; able to do this because I am alone. Before Mass I use a small copy of the New Testament and the Psalms belonging to Fr Tom McKenna who had been my constant companion until he sustained injuries in the mountains of Madeira some two years ago. It is a tiny book and light, which is essential for one who carries a rucksack.

Inside the fly leaf is written:

T.G. McKenna   GR 10 Pyrenees June 1977
                GR 5 Vosges September 1980
                GR 4 Auvergne 1982
                Offa's Dyke June 1983
                Austria Subaital June–July 1984.

– testimony to the companionship which saw us through so many wonderful holidays together. The GR is the symbol of the French 'Sentier de Grande Randonée', meaning a long distance footpath. Tom had introduced me to so much of this; ordered the tents and the sleeping bags, ordered the maps and the books. He was a secretary to several Archbishops of Liverpool and oversaw the rising of the new Cathedral from the window of his flat in the Curial Office. He was the first Administrator of the Cathedral and while still there organized me to join him in traversing the Pennine Way in sixteen and a half days; it was this which opened up for me the beauty of the moors and the hills of northern England. I have thanked God for it ever since.

14

I use the Psalms slowly because they speak to me of the journey I am on at present, with their praise of God for the beauty of the world and their appeals to God for protection. I then read slowly some of St Paul's Epistle to the Romans; and some short bits of the Gospel of Luke. They give me material for a reflection during the day. Then I say Mass. Slowly. I feel the wonder of his presence in this ancient inn beside a Pennine lake. I feel surrounded by the saints of Kirkby and the angels who guard me. I know Him, the crucified, risen victim. I receive Him as he told me to and only because He said it. And the mystery and the wonder of it remain as a background to the moors and the sheep and the wind and the rain.

There were three Americans at breakfast, they were cyclists. Ages? I would guess in their late fifties, tall and gangling, and they talked rather loudly so it was impossible to be a deaf toast-and-marmalade eater. They were cycling to the Lakes. They had been everywhere because of various business deals. They kept dropping the names of various countries in Europe and Asia and of multitudinous States in the US: they had been business consultants and engineers, market researchers; all up to date and technological.

I like Americans. They are usually so open and friendly, but they do seem to be everywhere. On our last night on the Pennine Way, Tom and I had found refuge in a disused railway truck, standing incongruously on a mountain side in the Cheviots some fifteen miles from Kirk Yetholm. We had settled down on the floor using the rucksack as a pillow; we had no sleeping bags and it was cold. Sometime just after nightfall the heavy ancient door slid open and a man came in with a girl. They settled down, brewed coffee and poured whisky into it; we were half asleep, so they did not offer us any. He was a Yank.

They crop up in the most unlikely places and I admire them for it; they have the freedom and versatility of a young nation and probably the means to express it.

I took a lift back to Egerton to the beginning of the footpath across the moor to Chapeltown. It was a glorious day. The sun was shining in a blue sky, with that lovely Pennine wind blowing over the moors, the sheep, and the grass so green, and the birds singing in the sky. My foot was hurting me, but

15

I felt fresh and confident. At Chapeltown I moved on to Turton Bottom and looked for a path which the map told me would lead to the footpath over the next moorland to the outskirts of Ramsbottom. It was not easy to find, so I looked for someone who could direct me and ran right into one of the frustrations of modern life. No one walks! Here was this exquisite village in the Pennines and the inhabitants were moving past me in cars. Woman with baskets going to some distant supermarket, children being driven to school, trucks rumbling past to deliver orders. The pavements were empty. I sat down on a wall and worked it out. There would be two classes. One would be men going for the morning paper. They had vanished by now. It was 10.30 a.m. They were back in their homes, reading. The other would be dog walkers. Dogs demand to be walked. I waited maybe half an hour and sure enough, a woman emerged with a dog. She had lived there for eight years. She did not know the way, but she pointed to a third class I had overlooked . . . the women hanging out washing. I approached one and she gave me explicit directions, and I began my journey to Ramsbottom. The path ran out, I took to the road and by one o'clock was in Ramsbottom. My foot was paining and the pain was becoming acute. I felt exhausted, even my legs seemed to have no strength in them. I went to a large central public house, ordered a soup and sandwich meal, and decided I would have to stay in Ramsbottom because I felt I could not go on. The hotel advertized accommodation, but when I asked for a room for the night, they replied they were full. They suggested other places, but I knew then that I would have to find the strength from somewhere: I did not want to stay in Ramsbottom.

I would walk over Harden Moor to Rochdale . . . a journey of twelve miles. I had already walked eight miles and felt exhausted, but I left Ramsbottom and began the Sorrowful decades of the rosary.

The path over Harden Moor leads to the A680, and at the junction of the path and the road there is a stone cottage standing high up on the moorland amidst the bracken and the flocks of sheep, and this day the wind was blowing gently upon it, and the late afternoon sun burnished the grey stones. I sat on a wall and took off the boot and put on yet another plaster. As I did so a bus passed making for Rochdale. I looked at it. It was like Satan in the desert telling Christ to make stones into bread. All my resolutions about pilgrimages faded and I signalled to the driver. He made a gesture which I could not interpret, and it went down the road in a cloud of dust.

A woman came to the door of the cottage. She was tall and slender with a white blouse and a blue skirt. I was putting a foam-rubber pad over the plaster, and I hailed her from the opposite side of the road, still suffering from the acute wound of human weakness opened up by the passing bus. 'Please,' I asked, 'can you tell me, when does the next bus come?' 'It will be three hours from now,' she said, 'if it comes at all.' I said, 'How far is it to Rochdale?' She said, 'It's eight miles', then added, 'but it's all down hill.' Somehow I lifted the rucksack on my back; the evening sun was sending rays of pity on the Ashworth reservoir, and three hours later I was in the centre of Rochdale. The pub at the town centre could not take me, but told me about a nearby hotel that would. I limped into it. The lady behind the desk said, 'It will be £40. Bed and Breakfast.' I pulled out a credit card, thinking, 'Sleep now and pay later.' I knew I was on a slippery path that leads to the bailiffs. 'I want to go to Mass tomorrow because it's Sunday,' I said. She looked at me. It must have been a long time since anyone had asked her that. 'The Catholic Church is nearby,' she said. 'I will let you know the times of the Mass later.' She looked at me, five foot two of pain and exhaustion; 'You can have the room for £25.' 'Can I stay for two nights?' I asked. 'You can,' she said. I couldn't kiss her because there was a big wooden desk between us.

17

Chapter 5

Rochdale and the Pennine Way

Rochdale is an unusual town. It stands in a valley between the
low peat hills which are like running noses feeding the two
small rivers which meet beneath and around Rochdale. It was
a central point in the Industrial Revolution in Britain, and the
textile mills which are dotted around the town and in the areas
adjacent bear witness to it. As East Anglia and the wool trade
laid the foundation of English prosperity in the Middle Ages,
the cotton mills of the Lancashire and Derbyshire hills were
the starting point of the prosperity of the Britain of the early
nineteenth century and later, well into the 1920s. I have
always associated Rochdale with this mill town image, which
I now know has gone and may never return.

I had associated it with Gracie Fields and 'She's a lassie
from Lancashire, just a lassie from Lancashire . . . though she
dresses in clogs and shawl, she's the prettiest of them all . . .'

I knew the song from childhood. It brought back memories
of my years as a priest, in Ashton-in-Makerfield near Wigan.
I was put in charge of the Girls' Club. I knew nothing about
girls; I had gone to a seminary at the age of eleven, had only
met girls in the short holiday season, and they kept their
distance and I kept mine. Deep down I was scared of them. I
think they knew it; they were very kind to me, gentle, helpful.
A big nun presided over the weekly meetings and part of the
time they sat around knitting. It was 1942–3 and a different
world. Now, these girls did wear clogs. They went off early
in the morning to a mill at the centre of Ashton, or to work
in the canteens of the coal mines, sometimes picking coal on
the outside of the workings.

They did not go down the pit. Some of them worked in munitions. They changed out of clogs and shawls as soon as they arrived home. When I think of them I regret the condom culture of our time, which has done so much to destroy the innocence of girlhood, and produced the fear of walking on the street even in daylight. One of the privileges, and the agony, of being a priest for fifty-four years is to have been so closely associated with the light and darkness in the very secret inner recesses of the minds of young men and women, as the war years and post-war years pressurized them into conformity with a different vision of society.

I went to Mass in the local church. It was a beautiful building, elegant externally, with a spacious dome over the transept and a sanctuary adorned with a magnificent mosaic. The Mass was at 10 o'clock and it was crowded. I hoped to be anonymous in the crowd as they entered into the mystery of Consecration, sign of Peace and Holy Communion. The parish priest seemed to be very young. That impression dates me rather than him.

At the end of the Mass I thought I had better introduce myself. He immediately asked me to wait for him in the presbytery and share lunch with him. I was deeply grateful. I suddenly realized that I needed to talk to a brother priest. He was on my wavelength.

We talked a lot about the parish. The church had been built in more spacious days when wealthy merchants of Rochdale built grand houses in the vicinity, days of full employment and before the mills closed one by one under the impact of new technology and the arrival of the multi-nationals. Margaret Thatcher's market forces had sounded the death knell. The old inhabitants moved out. The houses became flats and bedsits.

The shops closed and were reopened as takeaways and off-licences, and a flood of single parents and other cultures moved in. I knew the feeling; he was a young man alone in a big house in an advancing slum. It was difficult to form a pastoral plan other than plugging holes in dykes.

I was fortunate when I was in Kirkby. It was a comparatively new area. It was not yet a slum, although parts of it were deteriorating fast, especially the flats, high-rise and otherwise. But I had two priests to work with me, a church also new; a social club, an infant and junior school and two comprehensive schools for eleven-year-olds upwards which I shared with other parishes; one for girls and one for boys, with eighteen hundred pupils roughly in each.

There were one thousand three hundred Catholic homes in the parish, and approximately five thousand potential Mass-goers; about eleven hundred attended each weekend. The other asset was that it was all one social class. No one owned a house; they were all council dwellers. There was division between supporters of Everton or Liverpool FC, and the fact that half the population was nominally Anglican, but that was a minor division compared with the first!

The pastoral plan was comparatively simple, and it was possible because we three priests lived together, ate together, had just one television screen, and had a housekeeper named Ida, and a dog. The plan was based on three factors.

1. The visitation of thirty homes each, every week (except holiday periods).
2. The keeping of precise record cards.
3. A regular meeting to discuss case histories as they unfolded and determine the action that would be required.

The visitation followed a set pattern: Asking permission to enter the home; asking permission to make notes of names, children's dates of birth, schools; asking the jobs (if any) of parents. After that it was a question of listening to any problems that the family wished to present; discussion about spiritual issues, like prayers in the home, reception of sacraments and so on. But the main effect was to affirm the parents and the children, to make them aware that we cared. They were important, valuable. It was exhausting work, done mostly in the evening, three nights a week, between 5 p.m. and 9 p.m.

The card had been designed by a layman from one of the previous parishes I had worked in. Names, addresses, year of children's birth, school details, employment details, special notes for the priest's assessment of the situation involved, date of visit. The cards were kept in order in a large filing cabinet and were never seen except by the priests in the house and the layman who had shared in the planning of the scheme and the printing of the cards. This file became invaluable to me as the years passed and I had less help.

Every year Bob (the layman) obtained a copy of the voters' register, noted the changes from the previous voters' register and asked the Legion of Mary to call to ascertain whether the new residents were Catholics or not. That involved further visits by us, but meant that we were on top of a very fluid situation. Each year two hundred and fifty families moved in and out: it was an astonishing statistic.

The third element was the reflection on the case histories and the action taken. This led to the formation of a strong parish council; the forming of a Flat Dweller Group to get justice for hundreds who were trapped in flats. It was my initiation into the politics of the area. But I liked challenges. The Flat Dwellers became a strong instrument for change. So arose the 'Crisis for Kids' committee ... for the young men that were being hounded by the police; a Care for the Aged group, a liturgy group. Groups sprang up and flourished. It was all very exciting. The North American College in Rome sent us deacons to be trained during their summer recess; so did the Diocese and the Kiltegan Fathers from Ireland. The house was full from July to October, with young men eager to learn pastoral theology in a vibrant but socially-deprived area, the Western equivalent of the Third World. Film-makers came ... BBC and ITV for programmes about unemployment, Credit Unions, Change in Inner Cities. They made their programmes and went.

We worked in school, hammering out new catechetical systems and supporting harassed R.E. Staff. It was exciting and fulfilling. I began to need an hour early in the morning each day before the Blessed Sacrament. I needed wisdom and I needed peace. There was no other way. It became my 'fix': I could not do without it.

The change in that situation came slowly. The supply of priests dried up. New pastoral formation groups at diocesan level produced programmes for everything, from the cradle to the grave. All they needed were men and women to work with them at parish level. This meant going to find volunteers and sending them off to the training courses.

21

By this time I was alone in the house. It was the late seventies and the beginning of the eighties. I had also been asked to take care of an adjoining parish. But by this time the men and women in the parish were growing very close to me. We all met in the house, we all met in the kitchen. Something new was growing, as I got older and was no longer able to cope with ninety homes each week as the old system fell apart.

Ecumenism also was a major help. As grave social problems arose in the area owing to the blight of unemployment, we more and more turned to our Anglican and Methodist brothers and sisters, and we shared together in the work of supporting the people in their strikes and their agony at the closure of factories and workshops.

But finally I had run out of energy. In all those years I had been so grateful for the precious gift of priesthood. No other calling in the world is like it; not medicine, not teaching, not law. In all the years I had never been lonely or bored. And as I listened to the young priest in Rochdale my heart bled for him. It's hard to become part of a community when it is a drifting one, a community of people with no unifying force. Girls with babies and no husbands, Muslims, Asian families who feel alienated from English life, young men unemployed with no foreseeable chance of a job, tempted by drugs and companionship in a pub which becomes a second home. But to be part of a community is most essential for the priest. Jesus dressed in the clothes of the poor, sitting on the ground surrounded by people: teaching them, in dialogue, healing them, bringing peace, and with no visible means of support. They were with Him when He ate and drank; they knew He ate the same food they did. He wasn't going to Sainsbury's whilst they went to Netto or Aldi. He was part of their work and their life. Yet He was different. Mysteriously different. 'Whom do men say I am?'

I remember sick calls to a house full of people. The old woman lying on a bed, the children, and the grandchildren. And the great-grandchildren. They all looked a bit like the old woman on the bed. The men outside in the summer nights drinking from cans. They had all come to see the death of the old woman. They loved her; she had loved them from infancy; they were desperate. They had the small table ready in the room, two candles lit, the daughters kneeling around the bed. I put down the Pyx and spoke. The old woman raised herself on the pillow, her eyes open with incredible joy, a smile on her lips, she reached out two skinny arms and took my head and pulled it towards herself. Then she kissed me in a way that seared my soul. She was saying, 'I love you Jesus'. When she died they all came back for the rosary the night before the Requiem. One of the daughters looked at the crowd stretching out into the night. 'You see all these people here?' she said. 'The only sin they commit is that they miss Mass. Please give us general absolution. We all want to go to communion tomorrow.'

Time and time again, ineffaceable images: children sitting on kerbsides asking if they could make their First Communion although they were at 'Protestant' schools, in the bus, at the town centre, in the shops, on the street corners, in the smoke filled atmosphere of the Club, standing on the Kop watching Liverpool... people asking for something 'Will you say a prayer for ...?' 'Can you light a candle for me?', 'Can I come and see you?'... There were times when I felt that I was being drowned by a sea of faces but, alternatively, I floated on the sea of their needs and affection. We had a Reconciliation Service once a month. It began with the first part of the Mass ... the readings, homily, pause for thought. Then I heard confessions on the sanctuary, usually helped by another priest, while the organ played Bach, Handel, hymns, the New World Symphony. They came and knelt and talked: talked of a vision of the sorrows and darkness of manhood and girlhood, and the agonies of men and women faced with impossible dilemmas. It was a vision of life from the inside of minds full of super-natural grace and peace. Awesome glimpses of the beauty of God in the souls of these precious men and women. Absolution, then Offertory; Consecration. The radiance of Communion and peace. It always transformed me. It was almost unbearable.

I looked at the other occupations and professions ... the truck drivers, the shop assistants, the social workers in their seminars, the young doctors trapped behind their computers, and marvelled that God had chosen me for this. But all that is part of the mystery.

The next day I celebrated Mass with Father Ged: he talked briefly about the pilgrimage I was making and why I was doing it. After Mass a man came and gave me four new white socks, with cushioned soles. 'You could use these,' he said. And as I left someone gave me an envelope. I took it, asked what it contained. I can't remember what was said, but when I opened it later that night it contained £50.

Chapter 6

The Pennine Way

The Pennine Way is a long-distance footpath that runs from Edale in Derbyshire to Kirk Yetholm in Scotland: something over 250 miles of footpath, mostly over 1000 feet above sea level, sometimes 2000 feet, and once over 3000 feet, making its way through desolate peat wastes, charming meadows and woodland, over limestone and dark millstone grit, alongside rivers and gorges. It is undoubtedly the premier long-distance footpath in Britain, and Tom and I walked it twenty-one years ago and fell in love with moorland and limestone, with sheep in high valleys, and the wind and rain which are all part of the challenge.

When I planned this pilgrimage, I had promised Our Lady I would walk it in thanksgiving, but that I would not include walking through busy towns and cities ... conurbations; and that it would include using available footpaths where this was possible. For that reason I had avoided the whole Manchester sprawl by heading north of Liverpool and Manchester, north of Bolton and Burnley, and later sliding carefully between Derby and Nottingham. This added a considerable number of miles to the journey, but it gave me the silences I needed.

On Monday, July 8th, Ged Barry took me to the edge of Littleborough, just outside Rochdale, and I said a fond farewell to him. He had left a deep impression on me, and his kindness had come just at the right time. I picked up the Pennine Way at a pub called the White Horse, just short of the spot where it climbs up on a spectacular Roman Road (which some say was a medieval road, and they're always arguing over something!) It was a beautiful day, white clouds

25

drifting through a blue sky, a warm west wind moving the bracken on the moors, the millstone grit under foot. This was my kind of country: even the rucksack was light; I had packed the left boot with pads and sponge material, and for a while the foot behaved itself. Up to the trig point on Blackstone Edge, and down to the footbridge over the motorway spanning the deep gash in the hills, with the stink and roar of the M62 rising up towards it, like one of those visions of hell that some mystics have talked about.

On the far side of the footbridge, past the radio mast, where the A672 winds between Halifax and Denshaw, there is a lay-by where a mobile café awaits the truck drivers and the walkers, and serves hot dogs and burgers. You can breathe in the aroma floating down the wind, as you can on the journey to Anfield for a home game on a frosty day in winter. I stopped and he sold me tea and sandwiches: as I sat on a grassy bank and ate them, big trucks kept turning in. The truck drivers are usually a decent crowd; so many of my Kirkby friends were in the profession; it's a lonely life, high up in the cab filled with sophisticated instruments, like under-paid airline pilots; and I can testify they get energy from hot dogs or burgers. The mobile proprietor knew them . . . 'Hullo Gary' . . . 'Hullo Charlie'. The scent of the burgers floated around me on the moorland. I shouldered the rucksack and moved into the silence and solitude of the high moors.

I was still thinking about Ged Barry. I think bishops have got to give a lot of support to young priests put in charge of difficult parishes like his. At his age, I do not think I could have coped. I was so fortunate to have the assistance of so many lay people: the Legion of Mary, the Young Christian Workers, the Cursillo Group, the men and women of the Unemployed Centre, the men and women of the Credit Union . . . all these dedicated people who cried alongside me at the burdens of the area I was in, with its multiple problems and growing poverty. Thanks be to God, they were my support, and I knew there was no substitute. The support a diocese can give is minimal. A bishop is tied up himself with programmes which are printed in the Catholic papers under the heading 'Bishop's Diary'. Support for a priest has to come from inside . . . from the community in which he lives and moves.

By noon I was at Standedge on the flat millstone ridge looking over the Castleshaw reservoir, with Dingle and Uppermill beyond, and towards the east the houses of Marsden. I stood by the Ammon Wrigley Memorial (he died in 1946 at the age of eighty-five. He was a writer and poet, in love with his native Saddleworth). Around me were the rocks carved into gargoyles by the wind and the rain. The sun was shining down on the scene, on the reservoir and the emerald-green valley that once was a Roman camp. I carried with me a cheap camera I had purchased from Dixon's the day before I left, and I snapped everything in sight, but none of those photographs came out. I had made a mistake when putting in the reel.

I dropped down to the deep cutting carrying the old road from Rochdale to Huddersfield, crossed the road and took a footpath to Marsden. Below me I saw a farm with a board swinging in the wind. I went down to investigate and found it was a declaration that Bed and Breakfast were available. I knocked on the door and a pleasant kind lady answered. Attached to the house was a barn fitted up with bunks and facilities for showering, washing, and cooking. The farm-house itself had limited accommodation which had already been taken. I put my rucksack on a bunk, explored the facilities, and went into the farm where the landlady provided an evening meal.

There was a wood and coal fire burning in the kitchen hearth, for the evening was chilly. We sat around the fire talking ... a tall grizzly man in his early fifties. He was fit, lean and rugged with blue eyes and a full head of hair. His wife was younger by some years, good-looking and tastefully dressed in casuals. He had once been a shepherd on the Scottish hills, and had an extensive knowledge of sheepdogs. In answer to their questions, I said I was a priest and was making a pilgrimage to Walsingham in Norfolk and that I had begun this some days back. Their son by his first marriage had left home like the young man in the story of the Prodigal Son, and for long periods they had lost contact with him; the father admitted that he had been angry with him and obviously felt guilty that his son had gone away from him. Some weeks before, his son had broken the silence. He was near

Huddersfield with a girl and left a phone number or an address, I cannot remember which. So they had come north, taken rooms in this farmhouse and told him they would be there.

We had a long discussion about what parents should do in cases like this, and I hoped I put over the orthodox view. While we were talking there was a knock at the kitchen door. It opened and a tall gangling youth stood framed in the doorway. It was a moment of breathless tension. Then he stepped forward and kissed his stepmother and wrapped himself in the arms of his father. I stepped into the adjacent room and closed the door behind me.

Chapter 7

Over Soldier's Lump and the Laddow Rocks

There was a dank mist over Saddleworth the next morning, and the prospect of the twisting muddy path over Soldier's Lump and the Laddow Rocks was less than inviting. Mrs Hussey (the landlady) made breakfast; she was a very good cook, and then set out to find me somewhere to stay for the night. She telephoned Crowden Youth Hostel, and all the B & Bs in the Crowden area. They all answered, 'No room'. She tried the availability of accommodation in Glossop, and received the same reply. Finally she had an offer from a farmhouse situated south of Glossop, and I assented because there was nothing else on offer.

It looked somewhat daunting because without checking it up accurately it looked like twenty miles over very rough country at present shrouded in mist, and my left foot was still paining me. For all this extended phoning, Mrs Hussey refused any payment; she and her husband saw me off with their good wishes. Later, I learned she had phoned that night to make sure I had arrived safely. They were such kind people. He had been a building contractor and had become disillusioned by the tension and competition of modern business and, with full agreement of his wife, left the comparative luxury of the south and bought this remote farmhouse in the south-western Pennines.

The path led alongside a series of reservoirs, showing signs of the effects of protracted drought, through the remote valley of Wessenden, where, in season, the rhododendrons provide a

29

glorious splash of colour up the steep moorland hills by the side of a sheer waterfall. The path then climbs out of the valley to a lonely road across the moors, still haunted by the memory of the children whose tortured remains were buried here so many years ago by Myra Hindley and her mad accomplice.

The murder case has never been forgotten. Discussion flares up every now and again in newspapers and television. Well; should repentant sinners be allowed reconciliation with society after long periods of imprisonment? Lord Longford said 'Yes' and he was the mouthpiece of those who believe that repentant sinners should be given the chance to make restitution by working in freedom for the good of the society they have injured. He argued that is the way God works and we should imitate Him, but many others disagree, and it is probable that Brady, as with Hindley, will die in captivity.

This particular day that lonely moorland road, wrapped in mist with the threat of rain, looked like the classic scene in the black-and-white version of *Great Expectations* where Pip meets the convict with chains on his legs in the graveyard.

I wandered up and down the tarmac looking for the signpost to the Pennine Way. It was midday, and I had forgotten to pack any food or drink. Suddenly through the mist I saw the shape of a white van in a lay-by. It was selling hot tea, hot coffee and sandwiches. I moved in fast. Fifteen minutes later, refreshed, I found the signpost, took a compass bearing and began the uphill journey to Soldier's Lump. The black peat top of this remote moor is one of the loneliest spots on the whole 250 miles of the Pennine Way. In dry weather it is like walking on the moon. In wet weather the black peat clings like mushy treacle. Somewhere in the middle of it all is a trig point, a white squat pillar standing out against the gritstone and the peat. I reached it about 2 p.m., took a further compass bearing towards Laddow Rocks and set off down hill. I met two girls at the top burdened down with tents and bulging rucksacks. We exchanged experiences and I pointed them the way to the path to Wessenden. Then I was alone with the silent mist settling over the peat and the rocks.

I was reminded of the Lough Derg experience. I do not know why I get immersed in my own thoughts so deeply; on this occasion it was phenomenal. I first went to Lough Derg in the late forties. I had bought a second-hand motor bike. The war had been over for some four years. I went to Dublin, said Mass in the Cathedral and saw the notice about Lough Derg in the porch and thought, 'I'll have a go at that'.

Eventually I reached it. It was an experience that entered deeply into my spiritual understanding and I have returned year after year. An island, in a remote lake in Donegal, surrounded by low hills and not a farm or domestic animal in sight. On the island is a large granite building, a church dedicated to St Patrick, given the status of 'Basilica' by some long-dead prelate. Also on the island, a small church dedicated to Our Lady, two huge hostels, one for men and one for women, also a large house to accommodate the priests who are the chaplains, and the various members of the female staff needed by the pilgrims.

It is a three-day pilgrimage. The pilgrims must be fasting from midnight of the day of entry. Nothing to eat or drink: water is the only concession. There is a small payment to be made at a kiosk by the lakeside, and a boat takes one across to the island. The boat will be full of people – many of them young, for the challenge of Lough Derg is attractive to youth. When the boat arrives the pilgrims remove their shoes and socks. This pilgrimage is totally barefoot and the feet are going to be exposed to rough stones, rocks (worn fairly smooth by now), and sometimes extreme cold and wetness. I first experienced and began to understand Celtic Christianity in Lough Derg, and I do think that anyone who is interested in the power of Celtic Christianity should make this journey. There are endless prayers ... but always the Hail Mary, and the Our Father and the Creed. The prayers are as restricted as the food and sleep. Prayers are said walking in circles over rocks and the remains of the cells of early anchorites. Prayers said ankle-deep in water at the edge of a lake lapping eerily against the stones. Prayers whispered clutching an iron crucifix fixed into the rock, whispering the Our Father and the Hail Mary by the side of a young girl, an old woman, a young man; side by side, dimly aware of human personalities and of the soft rain and wind ruffling the waters of the lake.

31

There is one meal a day at Lough Derg, black tea or black coffee and dry bread: a meal to last twenty-four hours. There are devotions, and there is a vigil which begins at ten o'clock on the first night, which stretches through the dark hours of the night and into the following day until ten o'clock the following night, when the exhausted pilgrim falls into a dreamless sleep on a bed in the Hostel. In between the devotions, the pilgrims talk, smoke and rest. Trying to keep awake, trying to forget hunger and cold. Often they would tell stories ... the reason why ... doctors, professors, cab drivers, repentant gunmen, broken women, students praying for exams, priests with dark problems, women radiant with inner peace, and likewise men who come, year after year, because Lough Derg is their life.

Then there are confessions, hundreds of confessions. So many times, year by year, I have heard confessions at Lough Derg, and I carry the memories of all that. I understand why Jesus loves the sinners as well as the saints. Then on the final day with the last of the penitential prayers, the sun breaks through the clouds and shines through the struggling leaves of the one tree, which stands by the last penitential bed, so often I could have stayed there for ever, feeling the incredible peace of God which wraps me up in a tiny parcel of joy.

The Lough Derg fast continues after leaving the island, until midnight.

The journey into the 'civilised' world is different because I have seen a world that is different. So when the people of St Joseph's offered to pay for me to go to the Holy Land, on the occasion of my Silver Jubilee, I replied, 'No; pay for me to go to Lough Derg.'

Three days before my Golden Jubilee in 1992, I went back there again for the twenty-fifth time, so that I would be ready to celebrate my fifty years of priesthood.

I thought of all of this quite deeply, as I made the journey alone up the narrow path towards Laddow Rocks in the mist of that day, because what I was doing now was something like it. My foot was more and more painful. As I came down to Crowden in the valley I took off my boot and put on more pads. I crossed the Crowden Brook and began the eight miles to Glossop. It was eight o'clock in the evening. It had been twenty exhausting miles, I found a telephone box and phoned the B & B: a female voice answered. 'Wait there and I will pick you up.' I was meeting one of the angels.

Chapter 8

The Dark Peak

She was a slightly-built lady with the ageless look of someone with deep inner peace. She had recognized me as the priest who had celebrated a Mass for healing before Christmas 1995, and she had been at that Mass. Like many priests of my theological background, I had been extremely suspicious of the Healing Movement. During our theology course we had 'discussed' the miracles of Christ and the early Church. I put the word 'discussed' in inverted commas, because we did not really discuss anything in those days. We attended lectures. This meant we were passive recipients of the wisdom of the textbook and the professor who used it, sometimes as a tool, sometimes as the total content of a lecture. The lecture would be in medieval Latin, so it would be a mistake to call it a discussion.

There were multiple obstacles to discussion; not just the lecture system and the language barrier, but also the fear of being thought unorthodox ... what they now call 'left wing', or, in those days, 'smelling of heresy'. So we swallowed wholesale daft things like 'Moses wrote the first five books of Scripture' ... and that was *proxima fidei*. Not quite as bad as that: the phase was something like 'the author of', but I still used to have this cartoon picture in mind of Moses in a tent in the Sinai Desert writing on papyrus scrolls, and wondering where he got them from. Or, that he wrote them on animal skins ... and then I had this image of a bearded Moses leaning out of his tent at night, yelling, 'Kill another cow'. That would set me wondering where all the cows came from? The greater question still: when did he get all the time to write all those books? I never dared to ask the professor in case he reported it to the Rector!

It all seems daft looking back on it some sixty years on, but that is how it was, with me anyway. For instance we had spent some months on the tract *De Matrimonio*, about marriage. I was twenty-three years old and a year off ordination. I knew the tract *De Matrimonio* and found it incredibly boring: all those rules and hoops that people had to jump through to receive a sacrament, and the bad things that happened if they missed out. I knew since the age of nineteen or so that 'a baby was formed in the womb of a mother', but I had never bothered asking how the baby got in! I had no deep curiosity about it, being too caught up with other things.

It was one of the newly-ordained priests who told me how it all happened, just before the diaconate and some months after I had received top marks for my exam which included a three-hour paper on *De Matrimonio*. So I passed that exam with top marks, months before I knew anything about the central fact of marriage.

So it was with the miraculous. We were taught that miracles were needed in the early ages of the Church, because the world was pagan and the pagans had to be convinced by mega miracles. So – they said – Jesus and the apostles used that method, but when the world became Christian such visible signs were not needed. They surfaced at times to prove the holiness of a saint or the authenticity of a shrine like Lourdes, but otherwise they were not on the Christian agenda. In fact, there was something slightly heretical about them. The Albigenses used them, the Cathars, then the Baptist Charismatic Groups and so on. No ... the decent Catholic kept away. Healing, physical healing, was the job of the doctor; and when Freud, Jung and Adler came on the scene, spiritual healing was also the job of the doctor.

The priest had a time-honoured role. After the doctor and the psychiatrist had finished with the patients, and said there was nothing to be done for them, the priest was called in and gave them 'the last rites', which was a signal to phone for a sympathetic undertaker. Not much like the Christ of the Gospel, but it ran in parallel with the *De Matrimonio* and

Moses with a quill pen and cow's blood scribbling frantically in a tent under a Sinai moon.

Somewhere it had all gone wrong, and deep inside me I knew it. The laying on of hands in the Gospel, the commission to anoint with oil and heal the sick as a sign of Faith which had been given to 'believers' (end of the Gospel of St Mark), had somehow been taken out of the care of 'the believers', and into the hands of 'the professionals'. So, only priests or bishops could do it.

And then the authors of textbooks looked at 'the sick' and narrowed them down to 'the dying'. God alone knows why they did that, but they did. Then they went a step further and said that as the soul does not leave the body for some time after death, it is lawful to anoint while the body is warm. So the oil of healing had changed into a stamp on a passport to heaven. And my first sick call had been to a miner brought up from the Old Boston pit near Ashton. He was lying in a morgue, lit by blue lamps.

He was lying on a slab, his trousers and boots caked in coal dust. A massive rock had split his skull like an eggshell. Two doctors moved the two halves of the skull back and forth, slowly, like a squelchy orange. I had never seen anything like this before and the room began to spin around me. I held on long enough to anoint what was left of his face. I escaped from the drama, managed to mount my bicycle and rode back through two red lights. The Canon looked at me and suggested I took a nip of whiskey, but I don't drink alcohol. That was the nadir. The healing power of Jesus Christ had just been bestowed on a poor miner lying on a slab, not for resurrection to this life, but to eternal life, and that was fair enough, but was that it?

Then some seven years ago Michael Buckley phoned me and asked, Could he celebrate a healing Mass at St Joseph's. I had known Michael for many years, but only distantly. He had been a curate in Leeds, when he began a system of parish missions call 'And you?'. (A poster asked the question 'Can you come as well?') I used the system with some effect in Woolton and in Kirkby, and he had been very helpful; I had taken groups to short courses in Woodhall when he was in charge. Years had passed since then, and now, out of the blue, he was phoning about a healing Mass. I said 'Yes' without hesitation, and a few weeks later he came.

To my astonishment the church was overflowing. They came from everywhere. At the end of the Mass he exposed the Blessed Sacrament and moved among the people laying hands on them. It was overwhelming . . . the feeling of Faith in the church, the sight of this man moving among the crowds of sick and troubled people. This was different; it was a scene straight from the pages of the Gospel and instinctively I knew it was right! I did not think that I should do it. I did not want that kind of notoriety, definitely not that; but he said I should and reluctantly at first I was pulled in.

But deep down I knew the cost. I would have to be more empty if Christ was to use me as an instrument. I would need that one hour of prayer. That year I joined him in the conference at Scarborough, and again I knew it was deeply the mission of the church and that I was part of it. So it all began. Then a group of lay people joined me, and John Shaw, one of the group, suggested a regular Wednesday night session of healing. I was incredulous and said it would not work, but I was willing to give it a try. Now some two and a half years on, more than ten thousand people have been through those healing sessions, and the number grows; cancers have receded; depressions lifted; hurts been healed; sight restored; hearing come back.

But in addition there have been healing Masses outside the Wednesday night sessions and one of them was at Glossop and that was how the slight lady in the car knew me that sunset evening in July 1996. The next morning I celebrated Mass on the table in her dining room and she radiated faith and devotion. The other members of the family did not come, but I did not query that. We talked for a long time at breakfast,. She gave me food for the journey and I took a photo before I left of her framed in the doorway. But, alas, it did not come out.

The heavy mist brooded over the Dark Peak, hiding the deep peat troughs and the gritstone which peeps out from the blackness. Kinder Scout is an acquired taste and I am not a devotee. I was glad I was not going over Bleaklow, but crossing by way of Hayfield, the Edale Cross and Jacob's Ladder, which is the alternative part of the Pennine Way. At Hayfield,

I followed the map and compass painstakingly; I could not afford to make a mistake, not on the Dark Peak, and I got it right. I had been wearing a little red hat up to this stage. Somewhere on Kinder it fell off and I could not find it. From then onwards to the end of the pilgrimage, the rain, sun and wind had access to the little hair that was left on my head. (But if anyone finds a little red hat on Kinder decorated with a leprechaun, please send it back to me.)

The Edale Cross stands on the western side of Kinder, high up against the surface of the rock. It is a relic of an earlier age of Christianity, but one comes across it quite suddenly in a mini-shrine at the side of the mountain path. It may be one of the crosses which were a feature of the ancient corpse roads; like the one between Haweswater and Shap Abbey in Cumbria, or the one which curves over the three-thousand-foot top of Cross Fell, I have not researched Edale Cross and I promised myself that I will do so sometime in the future. Meanwhile I took a photograph of it, which like the others on the reel did not come out.

Jacob's Ladder led steeply down hill. It was hard and stony and the pounding on the left foot was agonizing. But suddenly, I was below the mist walking on soft turf, and the sun was shining. The steep hillside, dotted with sheep, clear against the vivid green of the hills; the mist still swirling around the top of the Dark Peak and the sunshine dancing on Kinder river which tumbled along the valley floor far below. I forgot my foot and bathed in the beauty.

It was still comparatively early in the day and I had reached Derbyshire. I thanked the Lord that I had not had to cross Bleaklow but had crossed the mountain by the way of Hayfield.

I had booked a B & B at Barber Booth before leaving Glossop, I reached it at four o'clock. The lady was apologetic that she had no single room, and the double room was £18. I was happy with that; I changed into sandals and made myself a pot of tea, with the facilities provided in the bedroom.

Then I walked through the field to Edale. I needed to ascertain the easiest way to Matlock using footpaths; they rightly recommended the Limestone Way, which had recently opened between Castleton and Matlock. I saw it on the map and it looked right. I went to a hotel and had soup and a sandwich, went back to the B & B and climbed into bed.

At ten o'clock there was a knock on my bedroom door. The man of the house put his head apologetically around the door. A young Frenchman had asked for shelter for the night; he had tried everywhere and found no vacancies. Would it be possible for me ...? He was looking at the empty bed in the room! Of course, I said Yes.

The young man undressed and we talked. He was from Alsace-Lorraine. I asked him about the extraordinary wall they call 'le mur paien', which winds its way along the hillside of the Vosges high above the River Rhine. It was built in some pre- Christian era from huge blocks of stone; there is a tiny remnant of one like it in the Yorkshire Dales, and they call it the Celtic Wall.

We talked about the convent of Ste Clothilde, which stands above part of the wall high up in the Vosges, where Tom and I spent a September night in 1980. The young man had been there and had also been a guest for the night, but I did not mention the prophecy of Ste Clothilde which had appeared in *The Tablet* here in England, in the middle of the Second World War. It seemed in an uncanny way to outline the events of that war, culminating in the horrendous destruction of Hiroshima and Nagasaki, which the prophecy spoke of as 'the rays of the sun burning on the earth'. It was probably all coincidence, but the writing aroused a great deal of interest in the nineteen-forties. Clothilde had lived in the Middle Ages, before Adolf Hitler or anyone like him had entered human imagination. I guessed the young French lad would not have known these things because he was too young. Later, when I told my friends an Alsatian had knocked on my door at 10 p.m. and gone to bed in the empty bed next to mine, they thought I was joking.

Chapter 9

Derbyshire

I left Barber Booth in bright sunshine. It was 9.30 a.m. I had phoned Millers Dale and secured a night's lodging; it seemed to be within comfortable walking distance, so I could take my time, and finally the landlady had only charged me £14 because that was the price for sharing a double room. But in addition I was pre-occupied by my own thoughts, which led me to think of my encounter with the young Frenchman.

The Catholic priesthood has many inbuilt difficulties. When I was a young priest I had always to share a house with others. I had my own room, but everything else I had to share with others: the bathroom, television, the fixed mealtimes, the consultation necessary before any big event, or looking at pastoral objectives. And all this meant that apart from the needs of the people in the parish, I had to be thinking continually of the feeling of the people in the house. If we had made a decision in common about something, I could not change it, even if I though it was not as good as the one I thought up later. All this was constricting and it was good for me.

But now I am old, I have my own flat; and before I resigned I lived in a house with a lot of men, women and children in and out of it. But in the late evening I could turn up the gas fire, pick up a video or a programme on TV, or read a book or listen to music ... on my own; I ate when I wanted. I did not have to fit in with anyone. I could heap up as many things as I wanted around me. Books, tapes, cameras. Celibacy can breed selfishness. It is a major danger for a priest, because no-one seems to notice: only God.

If a priest becomes alcoholic, it is noticed and corrected

(sometimes too late). If he falls in love with a woman, it is noticed and becomes a scandal. But the most respected priest can heap up things around him and become totally selfish, and still remain 'respectable'.

Married people can't. The husband and wife have to consider each other all the way through marriage, and if they do not, the marriage either breaks up, or becomes a living misery. The children also break down walls of selfishness; they demand love, they demand selflessness on the part of a father and mother. If there is very little money the children get the food, the children get the clothes. The mother in particular goes hungry and shops for clothes at Oxfam.

Not long ago I went on holiday with a friend of mine who is a married priest. Because he is married he is not allowed to use his ministerial priesthood. He is now approaching middle age, and I knew him when he was a young priest working in the same parish as myself. I said to him, 'I think you are in many ways a better man now than you would have been if you had stayed in the ministry. If you had stayed, you would now have been a fat, self-satisfied bureaucrat, handing out instructions, advice and reproofs to passive congregations; whereas now you are patient, tolerant, unselfish and poor, and your wife and children have made you that way.'

He was a member of our healing team and I remarked that all his sacerdotal gifts were now being exercised except consecration of the bread and wine of the Mass, but they were coming from a different and purified source. He never forgot this conversation and referred to it time and time again, when we were alone. I said it because it is true, and that selfishness is a bigger danger to a priest than lack of chastity, for I can be chaste as an angel and as selfish as Satan.

The other side of this was security. In St Joseph's I was the richest person in the parish. I lived rent free in a big house, which was adequately furnished. My food was provided by the parish: heat, light, bed linen, cleaning materials ... they all came free to me. I had a pension from the State when I reached 65 and it came to some £50. No-one I knew in the parish had £50 a week pocket money. So many of them lived below the line drawn as the official poverty line.

They avoided shops like Marks and Spencer, would never

venture into Sainsbury's. Anyway, these shops do not open in areas like Kirkby; and I would not be willing to go inside their doors. The people travelled on bus or train, using Saveway tickets or an OAP Pass. They put aside each week something to cover gas and electricity and rent. They dressed in cheap clothes. They could not 'go out' to bingo or social clubs, except in a limited degree.

Young married couples with children were hard hit; they had to buy a house because the council houses were sold under Thatcher. They felt they could not have more than two children. They go out to work, man and woman, to keep the roof over their heads. Filling shelves at Asda on £2.80 per hour. Working at odd jobs around the district, cleaning windows, cleaning office blocks ... all on the insulting wages given to the voiceless poor. Wages, destined to be what they are, because John Major rejected the Social Contract of the Maastricht Treaty, and left the poor powerless against the greed of the rich!

I lived through all this and marvelled at the inner dignity of our people and their readiness to laugh in the face of the situation. But I often felt ashamed that I was secure and they were not. The men and women who used to discuss these things in our house 'pooh-poohed' my viewpoint, but I felt then and feel now that it is valid.

If I had not been so taken up with all this I might have got in earlier, but it was evening when I reached Millers Dale, in a remote part of Derbyshire hemmed in by limestone cliffs and luxuriant vegetation. Early that morning I phoned through to the owner of a cottage offering Bed and Breakfast.

The cottage was owned by a husband and wife who had come from Essex. He had been employed by British Telecom and obviously had a highly-paid and responsible job; she likewise had been a wage-earner; between them they had bought this exquisite cottage as living quarters, and very luxurious they were.

The downstairs area was providing accommodation for two guests. I had one of two rooms. The other was occupied by a young policeman and his wife or girl friend ... one never knows. They had come for a walking holiday and had been based at the cottage for some days. Mr McAuliffe, the proprietor, talked a good deal about the number of people who came to Millers Dale, for fell walking and nature study. 'We had a man here last week who was at least seventy,' he said, looking over his shoulder at his wife. 'He was seventy, wasn't he, dear?' 'I'd say he was nearly seventy-three,' she said, 'and went walking every day.' I agreed that it was unusual for a man that old to be abroad. They did not ask me my age, not then anyway

Mrs McAuliffe directed me to a local small hotel, which was renowned for its good food. I found it, but had to wait for it to open. It stood in a side lane, with a stream running in front of the hotel and parallel with the lane. It is an exceedingly beautiful area and so remote from the busy roads which I would encounter later. I enjoyed the meal, but it was nothing special. I ate chicken for the first time for years. I felt I needed more protein.

Chapter 10

Tragedy

I awoke in the silence of Millers Dale, long before the policeman had risen in the room opposite, or the young lady who
was with him. I had showered and celebrated Mass, had
breakfast, paid the account and was beginning to put on my
boots when the landlady came down with the receipt for the
money. I was at a point where my left foot was bare; she
looked at the pad soaked in pus and blood, and the sole of my
foot which was raw and bleeding slightly. She said, 'You can't
walk on that.'

I looked at her dumbly, because I knew she was right, but
I did not want to hear something that was right. I wanted to
move to the next stop. She called her husband. He looked at
it. 'You'll have to see a doctor,' he said. I saw no point in
arguing this, especially when he said, 'I'll take you to the
doctor.' He phoned up and said he was coming, in case there
was need to make an appointment.

The surgery was in Tideswell. It was a neat, low, bunga-
low-type building. The doctor was young, clinical; he wasted
no time, looked at my foot and said, 'It looks like you have a
major burn; the skin has peeled off the ball of your foot, but
the infection has gone. You can't walk on it; it has to be
rested.'

He sent me to the nurse, who dressed it. 'It will take two
weeks,' she said. I was deeply depressed. There was no point
in trying to stay in hotels or B & Bs; Mr McAuliffe slung all
my gear in the back of his car. I said good-bye to his wife and
he drove me to Buxton. I caught a train to Manchester,
phoned my friend Liam and took a train to Wigan. He took

me to his house in Wigan, then dropped me back at Upholland, and left me with dark thoughts. I only knew that I would go back to the place I had left, and from there I would walk to Walsingham.

Meanwhile, exhaustion at first anaesthetized my mind, I arranged to see my GP, who confirmed what had already been judged, that it would take time.

Among the letters which awaited me was one from Joanna Wilson, from the Remand Centre at Risley. She was one of three women who had illegally entered one of the hangars at the huge Salmesbury centre of British Aerospace and 'disarmed' a Hawk fighter plane painted in colours of the Indonesian air force. A fourth woman, part of the group, was also involved.

Subsequently they had been arrested and been in prison since January awaiting trial for the offence. Joanna wrote to me and asked me to be a character witness and the letter went more or less as follows.

It's impossible to say whether we would definitely call on you or when you would be needed. I hope that you don't mind the degree of uncertainty.

My guess is that character witnesses could be needed some time between Thursday 25th and Tuesday 30th July, though I expect we could work around your availability to some extent. The aim of calling character witnesses is to demonstrate that I am a responsible member of the community, a person of honesty and integrity. We applied for bail recently and had a hearing in front of our trial judge, Judge Wickham. He refused bail outright without so much as looking at our character references and £150,000 plus sureties! He said we were professional troublemakers and that he could 'put us away for a very long time'.

Our main legal defence is that we were 'using reasonable force to prevent a crime'. This is recognized as a proper legal defence under English law and spelt out in the Statute Law. We were trying to prevent the Indonesian Government from committing genocide against the people of East Timor and British Aerospace from being complicit in this crime of genocide. We also intend to present an international law defence (all people have a right and even a duty to prevent crimes against humanity) and a defence of necessity (an English Common Law defence). We will also state the very simple moral and ethical justification for our act of disarmament.

We believe our action was lawful as well as defensible in International Law. The judge may well disallow all our legal arguments and may even direct the Jury to convict us. Fortunately, Juries have more power than they often realize and have the right to acquit us whatever the Judge says.

The letter finished by going over the times and occasions when we had met.

I read the letter with a growing feeling of amazement; I had met Joanna on many occasions but had never really spoken intimately with her, or worked with her. She had been, I thought, a member of the Anglican Church. She challenged the Labour stronghold on the local council and as an Independent had been elected. People thought highly of her, but I did not know her in the way I know, for instance, Christine at the Unemployed Centre.

I thought the Rector, Anthony Hawley, would be better than me.

I also felt that it would be a long delay for me, longing, as I was, to resume the pilgrimage. I decided to see her in Risley and phoned the Catholic Chaplain who agreed to take me under his wing and arrange an interview with Joanna. It was fixed for July 19th. I met Aidan Kelly, the Chaplain, at one o'clock outside the main gate. Risley is surrounded by green fields. It is an ugly concrete obscenity in these surroundings, like the ugliness of rape. There is a Visitor Centre where relatives can wait, but I followed orders and went to the main gate, gave the name Aidan Kelly, and was allowed to remain and wait for him.

It was the time when the warders changed shifts and I saw them coming in. They all had to be checked in by a secu-

46

rity guard at a kiosk, who also handed out sets of keys to them. The Wardens were males and females. They seemed to me very beefy. They wore a uniform, white shirts and black trousers, with some kind of flash on the shirt and on the shoulders. They seemed to have boots on. Beefy, burly, red-faced, I felt sure they were tender parents to wife and children, to husband and children; gentle as doormice at home, popular in the locality. But somehow the buildings seemed to change them. The very concrete and bars seemed to emanate something. They looked at me curiously but said nothing, and vanished through the gate with bunches of keys hanging from their waists.

At one o'clock Fr Adrian came. We went together to his quarters. I was surprised that the courtyard inside the walls and the building themselves were so colourful. There were flowers growing in the courtyard and the section I entered was pleasant, bright and colourful; curtains and utility furniture. Fr Aidan told me that the few years under Governor Friel had changed the whole atmosphere of Risley.

Joanna came and we talked at length. She said that she and the other three woman (because four were involved although only three had broken into the Warton factory), had mentally accepted the possibility of a long sentence. I talked to her about inner peace and the necessity of no bitterness. What they had done was a courageous and merciful thing; she must not lose her inner peace and not give in to negative thinking. She said she had no strict attachment to any religion, but was attracted to the Quaker way of life with its silences in the presence of God and its outlook on peace and non-violence. This I thought was very encouraging. The Quakers are remarkable people.

The actual movement she was involved in was the Ploughshares Movement. I came across the movement in 1982. Knowsley Borough Council wanted to send a representative to a big disarmament conference at the United Nations, and they asked me to represent them as a member of a non-government organization. NGOs (as they are called) have a substantial role to play in matters of this kind. They come from many democratic societies and represent civilian and political movements of some consequence. I was given a sum of money to cover my fare to New York and my accommodation.

I had long been a member of Pax Christi. I was involved in campaigns against the arms trade and was well known in Knowsley for my opposition to nuclear weapons. I had for some years been of the opinion that nuclear weapons were evil, and could not comprehend why the official church had not condemned them.

There was all this talk about contraception and all kinds of strictures against it, but it was only a tiny thing in comparison with the nuclear weapons which could destroy the world, yet bishops and archbishops seemed to tolerate their existence. I was vocal about this and some my colleagues thought me to be very 'left wing'. But that was the least of my troubles. Anyway, Knowsley saw fit to send me to America to represent them; and they asked the Rev. John Stanley, the Rector of Huyton, to go with me. I had not met John before; he was not in any peace movement, but was happy to accept the duties required of an NGO. He thought that his bishop would arrange for him to stay in New York, but on the flight over he told me that nothing had been arranged.

I had been in contact with one of the priests in America, who had worked as a deacon in St Joseph's while he was a student at the North American College in Rome. He had phoned from New York to say he had secured a place for me in the Hayes Hotel. It was a building in Manhattan, half hotel, half hostel, for the benefit of visiting RCs like myself.

We arrived at Kennedy Airport and I phoned 'The Hayes' (named after the Cardinal). They told me a bedroom was arranged for me. I then said that I had another priest with me. This caused some consternation, they said there was no spare room. We went anyway, by taxi, it was midnight. The man in charge was an American of Scottish ancestry. I said I was from Liverpool. He put down his pen and looked at me. Then he said 'Do you know Kenny Dalglish?' I said, 'I see Kenny at every home game.' 'Sign here,' said my man. 'And we'll fix up a bed for the other priest.'

So we gained entry to Manhattan and the work of NGOs. Each day we walked over from West Side Manhattan to East River, across Times Square. We saw the sections of New

York where the pavements were broken and the shops were run down; and we saw the sections of New York in probably the richest square mile in the world. Opposite the United Nations building was the Ploughshares Building. The name had been given to it from the prophecy of Isaiah, 'They will turn their swords into ploughshares'. It was a tall building, with many rooms and facilities. The whole organization was dedicated to non-violent elimination of arms and warfare. I met Bruce Kent and others engaged in the battle against nuclear weapons. I met some old women, Quakers from Cornwall and the Western Isles, old women with white hair and gentle faces who had scraped and saved to come and do what little they could in the cause of peace.

It was a week which made a deep impression on me. We put the case for peace to Russian and American and British Embassies. They listened courteously, they gave us time. They explained their reasons for the stances they took. It was all very civilized, they knew we were tiny pawns. We were powerless, it was a symbolic act: but symbols are important; they are sacramental.

So when Joanna said she was in the Ploughshares movement. I knew precisely what she was saying.

Chapter 11

Trial and Pilgrimage

It was Tuesday, July 23rd when the trial began. I went down
to the High Court in Liverpool, a building I had not visited
before, and I was impressed. The lifts, the carpeted corridors,
the open space outside the courtrooms, the opportunity for
people to meet and talk and even smoke in comfortable
surroundings, the cafeteria – all these various aspects of the
large building were designed to make justice accessible for the
citizens. Outside there is a large open space, and it was decorated with crosses on which were written the names of people
who had died in the invasion of East Timor. There were
people holding banners and one of them was Arthur
Fitzgerald, one of our priests. A Buddhist nun dressed in
saffron robes sat in front of the door of the courts beating a
drum rhythmically. The trial had attracted a large number of
people and the attracted ones were predominantly Catholic,
from Justice and Peace groups, members of Pax Christi, and
so on Inside there was a waiting list for getting into the court
itself, but I was allowed in because I might be needed.

So began four fascinating days. Three of the women had
opted to conduct their own defence. Joanna had a barrister.
The barrister was a tall slender woman, dressed in the wig and
gown demanded by the occasion. The prosecuting barrister
was similarly dressed. He was male, and not as tall as the
defence barrister. The court was crowded and the four women
sat together. I sat next to Norma Nelson, the Anglican woman
priest who had also been asked to be a character witness.

The judge was scrupulously fair. He was extremely courteous. The jury was a mixed bunch of men and women of

differing age groups, and all were treated with great respect and thanked for undertaking this duty. From the beginning it became clear that there was no doubt in anyone's mind that the women had in fact broken into the hangar at Warton and damaged vital parts of a Hawk aircraft. They scattered seeds inside the cockpit, left a video on the seat to explain why they did what they did, wrapped the plane in banners and tried to attract the attention of the security with no success. The crowbar which they had used they had painted with bright colours and decorated with peace symbols, and the hammers had also been decorated to look like the kind of things you give for wedding presents. It was all very female, like the touches women give to a room and it looks different.

All this was cheerfully admitted, almost like they had been going to decorate the flat of a sick friend, instead of disarming a deadly weapon. And to all this they pleaded Not Guilty on the grounds that their action was designed to prevent crime. They had tried for five years every other approach, talking to diplomats and politicians, demonstrating outside embassies; approaching the Directors of British Aerospace ... an endless list of trying to stop the genocide of East Timor, all without success. So they said 'Not Guilty', and this had led to this trial in the High Court.

The prosecuting barrister had a problem. He had obviously been briefed to deal with three women guilty of criminal damage, and found himself faced with a trial that swung almost immediately in a different direction. It became a trial of British Aerospace's involvement in genocide, in a court full of visitors out of sympathy with his case. The agenda swung out of his control. It was firmly in the hand of the five women, one a barrister, the other four highly intelligent and motivated. The Judge was strictly neutral and the debate was conducted on a high level.

I met Joanna's parents. Her father had the academic look of a university lecturer. Her mother was a gentle person, obviously grateful for the spiritual support of Josie and Sadie and a large group of men and women from different parts of Liverpool who saw this as a trial of good against evil. In the next two days there were religious services at various churches in the district.

On Wednesday and Thursday I spent most of the day in court buying cups of tea during the breaks in the proceedings. On Thursday also, Joanna was in the dock for some hours and stood up well to questioning. Late in the proceedings on Thursday Norma and I were asked to testify and we did this. I did my best but had not expected to be called until Friday and had left my script at home. After I had done this I felt free to resume my pilgrimage and wrote to Joanna to tell her I would be praying for her in the days that followed. And I kept my promise to her. In the hours before and after the court proceedings I had been working on maps and getting addresses for bed and breakfast; I spent Friday buying materials I needed for the rest of the journey, and on Saturday at eleven o'clock I left to resume my pilgrimage. The trial was still on, but I was impelled to take to the road again.

Georgina from Kirkby drove me. We reached Matlock in the early afternoon, went to the Information Centre in Matlock and were informed that all accommodation in Matlock was taken. All hotels and farmhouses, and B & Bs in that fairly large area were already full. It was unnerving. Obviously we had to have two singles, and they were in the shortest supply. The Information Centre itself was thronged with visitors. Of course it was now the end of July. It was the holiday season and Matlock is at the heart of the Peak National Park.

The gentleman handling our application was a middle-aged man, a bespectacled individual, bald on top and very courteous. He went again to look to make sure of his facts and discovered a farmhouse some seven miles outside Matlock with two singles. There had been cancellations in a wedding party. We said, 'Book it.' It was a place called Crich. We went there and claimed our bedrooms and left our rucksacks. Then Georgina drove me to Youlgreave which is some twelve miles from Matlock and on the Limestone Way. She walked with me half way: she walked back to the car and met me as I entered Matlock. We began the walk at five o'clock; it was eight p.m. when we were reunited. We went in search of fish and chips and returned at ten p.m. to the farmhouse.

It had been a wonderful evening. The evening sun had filtered through a hazy mist; the uplands of the Limestone Way were a mass of heather and wild flowers. Without the rucksack I was moving swiftly, no pain now from my foot. I was wearing new boots bought me for me by the Community College, and there was a song in my heart. It was also refreshing to have a companion, and Georgina was ideal. She is a very tall girl, used to the mountains and moorland, a sister in the maternity unit at Fazakerley Hospital and glad of a break in what was, to her, new territory.

The next morning she came into my room and I celebrated Mass of the ninth Sunday after Pentecost. It was the Gospel of the Apostles walking through the cornfields on the Sabbath, and all around us here were fields of ripening corn. It was a joy to share the Mass with Georgina and we both felt uplifted. Georgina insisted on paying the bill for our short stay. Before I left, also, I phoned through to Belper and secured a night's lodging in the Chevin area of Belper, at the far side of the river in the hills, somewhat south of the main town and some eleven or twelve miles from Matlock.

After that we drove to Millers Dale to complete the missing ten miles between that and Youlgreave. This would make my pilgrimage complete, whole. I would have walked to Walsingham from Upholland.

The sky was threatening rain. We went into a tiny café and had tea and scones. Georgina posed on the road in front of the cottage from which I had been invalided home. It would have been a good picture if it had come out. But it didn't. Then we did a repeat of yesterday; Georgina walked halfway, then went back for the car, and I met her at Youlgreave. It was a comparatively easy ten miles, although some of it was tricky and some of it climbed quite high. When I reached Youlgreave I felt tired and would have been glad to call it a day. But it was not to be. We drove back to Matlock at 4.30 p.m. and the mist had settled down on the hills. This time I added an egg sandwich to the inevitable scones. I felt I needed something to give me a boost as I set out to Belper. Georgina drove ahead of me to a place called Ambergate in case I was not going to reach Belper. But I was moving and knew I would be all right. So she said goodbye, turned the car round, and vanished in the evening mist on the long journey back to Kirkby, leaving me alone with my thoughts and the chill of the evening. I was walking on the A6, one of the major roads which, mercifully, had a pavement; I said the rosary and immersed myself in the meditation, and ignored the swish of the cars moving past me, and the wind caused by the big trucks, spilling diesel fumes right into my nostrils. I reached Belper by nightfall, turned right at the traffic lights and went uphill at a left-hand bend to find the road in the Chevin, and came eventually to the cottage which had promised me accommodation.

A slightly built lady answered the door, welcomed me in, and I sat on a stool in the kitchen drinking tea and eating chocolate biscuits. Her husband came in and welcomed me. The lady vanished and the husband told me she was painting in the conservatory which had been added to the house. I imagined she was painting walls or something, but it transpired that she was an artist of no mean repute, with groups of people coming for lessons at various times in the week. Her husband offered me the use of the lounge in which I could watch television.

But television was not on my mind. I had travelled twenty-two miles on foot that day: I headed for the bedroom as soon as I had finished the tea and remembered nothing until the next morning.

Chapter 12

Between Derby and Nottingham

The next stage of the journey was one I had pondered over much in the planning. I was faced with two large sprawling conurbations, Derby and Nottingham, with the river Derwent being joined by the Trent. On the map it seemed clear that the rivers could only be crossed at certain places. In addition there are motorway barriers. Furthermore, the strip of open country between the two was quite narrow. I had spent hours poring over the maps to see how this could be fitted in to a pilgrimage which sought out secluded pathways, but also offered an opportunity for overnight accommodation.

I had drawn up a tentative route which required accommodation at a place in between the two major towns. I searched the book of B & Bs but there was no mention of anything in that area. So I borrowed the Catholic Directory and phoned the parish priest. Eventually I got him, after several attempts.

'I am a priest from Liverpool,' I said on the phone, 'and I am planning to walk to Walsingham from here. I am using B & Bs and hostels for accommodation. Please can you tell me if there is any accommodation in . . . (and I mentioned the area)?' Now, I thought, if there is accommodation there he will tell me. If there is not, he will say, 'Why don't you stay the night with me?' Because that is the kind of thing priests say to each other, and with some exceptions I have always found it so. And certainly when I was in Kirkby I always made the house available for priests who were passing, taking the night boat to Dublin or flying from Manchester. I consider the giving of hospitality a major virtue and a central part of the Christian message.

But this guy obviously did not think that way. He gave me two pubs he thought offered accommodation and rang off. I phoned the pubs and they did not offer accommodation.

Maybe the priest was having a bad morning or maybe he did not believe me . . . or maybe. But the fact is that it did not improve my view about the attractiveness of the organized English Catholic church, and added some affirmation to my theory that a lot of Catholics are not really lapsed, but they are not attracted by the cold and forbidding aspect of the Catholic community, and don't join them for the essential liturgy of the Mass.

However, the fact was that I had nowhere fixed where I was going to stay that night, but the lady of the house became for me one of the many guardian angels that I had met on this journey. She phoned relentlessly until it became clear that the only possibility was a place called Shardlow, some eighteen miles or so away, in a minor hotel called 'The Grey Lady'. And I settled for that. The artist also made up a packet of sandwiches so that I would have food for the day. All these little touches, like the tea and biscuits the night before, are all given free, and almost with affection, and it makes up for so much that is cold and forbidding in this world.

Oh when will we priests and religious realize that love and affection, and openness are gifts that God gives to make his presence visible in the world? And how can we attract the people hungry for Faith and lost in a wilderness of doubt if we do not show this face to them? Time and time again in the course of the journey, I have had time to think and reflect on the fifty-four years of my being an active priest, and the enormous lessons I have been taught by the people. For, just as in marriage the man influences the woman and the woman influences the man, so in a parish, the priest influences the people and the people influence the priest. And if people are not receptive of the priest or the priest of the people, then there is no dialogue, and something dies at the heart of the parish, even though the Mass is still offered there and the sacraments dispensed. New life does not spring from dead things. Somehow we priests have to set free the genius of the people to create new forms of service, new forms of spiritual expression. The old forms must always be renewed to answer the urgent needs of a fast-changing world. To block and forbid rarely creates new growth.

The tension in the European Catholic Church, and certainly in the Church of South America is partly due to the inability of a centralized authority to enter into a genuine dialogue with the people at grass-roots. The curtailing of liberation theology is a stark fact, whether its leaning towards Marxist philosophy is true or not, and whether that fear is justified or not. And the same seems to have happened with the base communities which came out of the theology.

Discernment is a rare gift. The history of the Church is littered with the wrecks of 'might-have-beens' like the Jesuit missions in Paraguay in the sixteenth and seventeenth centuries, or the original mission to China by the extraordinary Jesuit Matteo Ricci in the sixteenth century, the silencing of Teilhard de Chardin, and the muzzling of creative thinkers like Lagrange, de Lubac and Congar. Sometimes the Church seems to be lumbering along behind the rest of the world and making, later, frantic efforts to keep up. It is just a mysterious amalgam of human weakness and Divine Power. And anyone who reads it right can be absolutely certain that what Jesus says, 'I am with you always right to the end of time', is magnificently true. And without that the Catholic Church would long ago have ceased to exist. And I love the Catholic Church because we are all a bit like that.

I took the quiet road high up on the right-hand bank of the river Derwent, a road of shady trees protecting me from the hot summer sun. On the far side of the river the busy A6 was carrying the slow-moving serpent of little cars and big trucks. I felt alive and moved fast, because I knew it would be a long day. I was praying for Marie Swift who had undergone an operation for cancer, for John Keams who was very sick, and for the four women on trial. I offered the Joyful mysteries for them.

I crossed the river by the bridge and moved up a side road to Morley and out of it, on to a high moor. There was a golf course on both sides of the road. The Moorland Golf Club and foursomes were out, women and men, I watched, fascinated. I use to play golf, very badly. At one time I was a member of Royal Birkdale. I was a country member and paid initially six guineas a year. It rose to £120 a year, which was still wonderful value. I went with Tom on golfing holidays on the Fife coast in Scotland and on the Irish golf courses on the western seaboard of Ireland, where the huge Atlantic waves broke against the rocks far below the eighteenth green, and the wind curved the ball in a parabola towards the waiting sea. I enjoyed it, bad as I was at it. But gradually the lure of the hills and moors took over, and one season Tom became uneasy because the Royal Birkdale seemed to have some kind of anti Semitic attitude, not put in writing but actually existing. He wrote to them. They did not answer the question and he resigned. I did as well, but my grounds were different. No one in Kirkby could afford Royal Birkdale or would be admitted, so I felt I should be part of the community I lived with. The committee wrote to me a very kind letter accepting my resignation. Throughout our membership we had always been treated with great courtesy and kindness. Anyway, I was still fascinated to see others struggling on this beautiful day on the high moorland course.

I stopped to eat sandwiches in a field between the golf course and Stanley. The air was fresh, the air of the high moors sweetened by the heather and the gorse; the sun was shining as I sat there by the side of the path and ate the sandwiches prepared by the artist of Chevin, salmon and tomatoes and crusty brown bread. There was tea in a flask and the birds were singing in the hedge behind my back. Oh, I felt good, and feeling like that I decided to have one of the small café crème cigars of Monsieur Henri Winterman. I had the tin of little cigars, but could not find the lighter. I sat there pondering. I am not deeply addicted ... but there was something about that day! But, alas, no lighter.

Then I remembered the tiny magnifying glass that Georgina had given me for map reading. I took it out, waiting for a shaft of sunlight, focused it on the end of the cigar, and was enthralled to see smoke curling up from it. The last time I had done that must have been sixty years ago when I was in the Cubs. But, need I say it, I didn't do it then to light a cigar. I pulled out the map and looked at what I had envisaged to be the worst section of the walk. It was this. I had sought for some kind of open country between the ominous conurbations of Derby and Nottingham which spilled, hungry and ugly, across the face of the map; and it looked as though I might succeed. Ahead of me lay Stanley, a small village, and then Dale Abbey, and there seemed to be a pathway from Dale Abbey running straight down the map to the canal country, crossing rivers and passing under the concrete sprawl of the motorway.

As I was reading all this, a young man and his wife and children came into view, crossing the stile which lead to my path. I hailed them as they passed and they came over to me. On being questioned I said I was from Liverpool. The young man said he was from Birkenhead;[*] he told me he lived in Stanley, that their house was at the end of the path, and that they would have a cup of tea ready for me when I reached the house. It was a chance too good to miss, and I accepted, even though I realised that some eighteen miles lay between me and the bed I had booked for the night. They passed on. I repacked the rucksack, took a photograph (which did not come out) and took the path to Stanley.

They lived in a semi-detached house at the edge of the village, and I sat in the trim garden drinking tea and eating biscuits. He told me about his move to Stanley and the gift of the open country, especially for the children. He did not want them brought up in Birkenhead. I told him that I was a priest and I was walking to Walsingham. He asked my age and seemed astonished. I am not sure that they understood the idea of pilgrimage. They filled my flask with ice-cold lemonade, and I said goodbye with thanks.

(Sometime later in the year towards the end of September I was in my room typing this very account, and was, strangely, at this very point in it ,when the family arrived at the College and asked if they could see me. The security man on duty thought I was out and did not know when I would return. So they left their name, address and telephone number; and I have since been in communication with them.)

I took the path to Dale Abbey. The village gets its name from the abbey which, so the legend goes, came into being because a hermit lived in a cave near the hamlet. In a vision,

[*]Birkenhead is a part of Merseyside.

so the story goes, he was told to build a church there. The church became an abbey. It was destroyed at the Reformation and the stones were used to build some of the houses of the yeomen of the area. I took a photograph of the remains of the abbey. I photographed a wall and house which could have been built from the ruins of the abbey, for the stone looked as though it had once had a different home. I then tried to reach the site of the cave. There were stiles and waymarks but they pointed to some kind of jungle and led nowhere.

So I returned to the centre of Dale Abbey, and eventually found the central path I was looking for. It was a broad path which ran across a high plateau. On the left I could see distant houses in the suburbs of Birmingham. On the right, the cooling towers of some industrial plant on the outskirts of Derby. I was high above them, on this path which ran in a straight line for miles towards the distant silver of the river Trent. The day was sultry, cloudy with odd rays of sunshine coming through. There was scarcely a breath of wind, the temperature was somewhere in the eighties, and I began to perspire, which was rare for me and it went through my shirt into my rucksack. I thanked God for the ice-cold drink of my friends in Stanley. I was saying the Sorrowful decades of the rosary and the meditation merged into a picture of the child, about seven years old, who was part of the family I had left, and the memories of the first communion in Kirkby.

The first communion period had become something of a nightmare for me. In fact its imminence had been one of the reasons why I had retired at Easter before the first communion round began. When I was a young priest it was a time of real spiritual delight. The boys in their grey pants and white shirts, the little girls in veils and white dresses: the resurgence of the Faith in the parents. The crowds that came to confession after years away from the sacraments. The joy and the celebration in the springtime with the May blossom on the trees and everything coming alive.

It was like that when I first went to Kirkby in 1966, and had been like that in Woolton in the years preceding my appointment. I made a film about it, with a commentary by a teacher named John Farrell who taught drama, elocution and used beautiful words and conjured up poetical images linking the film into Faith in the true Presence. I used the film for parents' meetings, and to help their reflection on this big event in their family. At that time there was no fixed course for preparation and, probably, it was not needed. Later we used the Christine Brusselmann system which involved the use of catechists drawn from the parish, special liturgies, many parent meetings and an early start in late October. They were exciting times. The catechists were mostly young mothers who felt honoured to be given this responsibility. They were given a short training in holding the attention of young children, and they already had experienced something of this because of their own family commitments. The children once a month used the parish house, which was the house where I lived. Once a month every room except my bedroom was taken over by groups of tiny children with their catechists, and they loved it. The parents had their separate meetings, usually on a previous evening. The infant school played its part in the process; it all came together in a Saturday evening Mass where the liturgy was totally child-centred and focused on one of their themes, such as belonging, or making peace.

But no matter how well the course ran, no matter how enthusiastically the parents co-operated in it, after the big day of the first communion was over the parents resumed their normal lives and the children lost contact with the church. The pressures of the outside world were too great.

It began to show ominously at the end of the seventies. At that time parents began booking halls, clubs, and post-communion celebrations. The women concentrated more and more on the garish clothing for the little girls. The men concentrated more on getting the ale. The kids were dressed like princesses. The loan sharks had a field day. The parents on the dole borrowed up to £300 for a daft dress for the girls and Lord Fauntleroy gear for the boys. They therefore wanted a ceremony where the children could be seen up front, catwalk stuff. Readings for the Mass, music, silence, and prayer did not fit in. Something like a Carmelite convent in the Kop at Anfield.

The neighbours came; aunts and uncles who had not met the family for years turned up. Loud greetings were exchanged and sometimes in the middle of that uproar the Mass would start. The musicians did their best. Brief silence while a little girl in a white dress would read something from Scripture. Brief silence while the children sang a hymn. A gospel and then a slowly increasing uproar while the Eucharistic Prayer got under way. Communion, a prayer and a hymn, and then a rush for cameras, and I ran for cover from the noise and confusion. For the guests at the Last Supper the real business began as they parted to their separate discos, bouncy castles and cakes. The adults retired for a drinking session, chicken legs, meat pies, sandwiches and lager. I felt like an alien. Maybe I was getting old. It was a different world and I did not fit into it.

One year I put a video camera in the choir loft at the back of the church, and another, a camcorder hidden under a cloth on the altar. I edited the result into a composite fifteen-minute film, and showed it to the parents in the following October at the first of the parents' meetings. They looked at it in dead silence and said, 'We can't believe it. It must not be like that that': and that year they all agreed to have the Masses on Saturday evening, and things began to improve.

Later the diocese introduced a new syllabus and ruled out the use of the Christine Brusselmann system in the infant school. And for me it was the end of the road. But the extraordinary thing is that out of the ashes of those years, when the parents went west and I went east, there will emerge adolescents and then young couples who will live and die for a Faith that somehow was planted deep in the soul of a tiny child in the midst of all that noise and confusion.

Because the Holy Ghost over the bent
   World broods with a warm breast and with ah! bright
   wings.

So I pursued the Sorrowful decades of the rosary on the sultry day on a high plateau between Derby and Nottingham and with wild flowers on the side of the road looking up at me.

Chapter 13

Middle England

I came to the B5010 leading to Borrowash. But I had no inter-est in Borrowash, found an underpass beneath the A52 and a very quiet road down to Draycott. It was evening now, and I thought about a light meal that would give me energy to reach Shardlow. The only feeding-troughs in Draycott seemed to be Chinese or Indian takeaways.

So I found a pub and ordered myself a blackcurrant and lemonade. The pub did not serve food and the barmaid told me it was takeaways or nothing. I mourn the passing of the little cafés that used to sell hot muffins, toasted tea cakes, egg and chips, egg and toast. Their absence is another sign of a growing culture of rootlessness in which people walk down a street with a companion, dipping into plastic dishes holding some kind of aromatic mess. Like the sheep on the fells in winter dipping into winter feed dropped by a tractor in a field.

In the vanishing café, people could sit and talk over tea and coffee; and smoke if they wanted to do so. It may be that the modern neurosis about smoking has pushed the addicts on to the streets with plastic takeaways and closed down the cafés. But it is a loss to civilization, like the going of the London coffee houses which were the haunt of Samuel Johnson and his Boswell, or the Paris cafés which became the haunt of Samuel Beckett.

But at least the long ice-cold drink in the pub sufficed for me, and it saw me on the road via Church Wilne, a footbridge across the River Derwent, and a footpath that led straight into Shardlow and the Grey Lady.

It had been a long day. I guess it was well over twenty

miles, and I was glad to accept that the price would be £35 for bed and breakfast in this two-star hotel at which I was, that night, the only guest. I suspect that the name came from Lady Jane Grey, one of Henry VIII's victims. I was told that she lived in a manor house near Shardlow, and that it was from here that she accepted the ill-fated offer to become the bride of old Blue Beard. This is something I have not been able to verify. I can however provide the useless information that the Grey Lady does not normally provide evening meals, and I went to the pub across the road for soup and bread and an ice cream.

There was an air of opulence about the pub and its clients. The ladies had poise and elegance, the men looked as if they had stepped out of Brideshead; all wearing casuals of course, but that did nothing to disguise their quality, for even the casuals were expensive. And they communicated with each other in a non-obtrusive way, quietly and confidently. I was too tired to feel anything but tired. I enjoyed the affluent and soporific atmosphere and staggered across the road to my bed in the Grey Lady before night finally set in.

I woke up to grey lowering skies: no wind, and temperatures climbing to the seventies. I showered and celebrated Mass. I thought that I had overslept, that I awoke at 8 a.m, when in fact it was still only 6 a.m. So I meditated on the Gospel of St Luke and read the psalms in the little book that Tom McKenna had lent me – the book I mentioned which had written on the flyleaf the various walks we had done together in France and Britain.

It was still too early for breakfast, which I had asked for eight o'clock, so I talked my impressions of the pilgrimage into my memo taker. I knew I was tired despite a night's sleep, which had felt more like an injection of morphine than slumber. I did not know how long I could go on like this, to begin the day's journey afraid that I could not finish it. Usually the tiredness began to go as my stiff muscles loosened up and my spirits began to rise. Anyway, it was a pilgrimage, not a holiday.

I came back and back to the Lough Derg experience. I had long periods of silence especially on the footpaths and I sank deeply into myself, meditating particularly on the Church as I had seen it in the parish of the past thirty years with the endless ups and downs of the apostolate. I could see more and more the power of the Holy Spirit at work in that urban parish with its simplicity of life and death, with its acceptance of poverty, its love and generosity. I meditated on the subculture of men and women who lived well below the poverty line as defined by the national statistics, and the children who were going to be casualties in the world that was opening out before them. Sometimes it came from the rosary I was saying, but often it was part of the rhythm of my moving feet and the swinging of the rucksack on my back. I was a bit like King Alfred in Chesterton's *Ballad of the White Horse*.

> Fearfully plain the flowers grew,
>   Like the child's book to read,
> Or like a friend's face seen in a glass;
> He looked; and there Our Lady was,
> She stood and stroked the tall live grass
>   As a man strokes his steed.

> Her face was like an open word
>   When brave men speak and choose,
> The very colours of her coat
>   Were better than good news.

> She spoke not, nor turned not,
>   Nor any sign she cast,
> Only she stood up straight and free,
> Between the flowers in Athelney,
>   And the river running past.

So often the ballad matched my mood on this pilgrimage and I found myself quoting bits of it, because it was in its own way a mirror of my life in the past thirty years.

In terms of success or achievement, it had only been a disaster, measured, that is, in human terms. The kind of terms defined by phrases like 'Management by Objectives'. Mother Church kept me on. Industry would have sacked me long ago. One simple statistic: when I first went to St Joseph's, more than one thousand people attended Mass each Sunday. When

I left, barely three hundred, and most of them were old. In 1966 children and adolescents were a considerable part of the crowd. When I left, there were very few. But I never lost heart, and for most of the Pennine section of this pilgrimage I sang *Veni, Sancte Spiritus*, to the wind and rain on the moors which stretched from Blackstone Edge to Kinder Scout.

I wondered, that morning in Shardlow in the interval between Mass and breakfast in the Grey Lady, if anyone I had talked to on this pilgrimage had the remotest idea of what I talked about when I said I was making a pilgrimage to Walsingham. There seemed to be so little understanding of my religious theme. I remarked to my memo taker about the kind people in Stanley, that lovely young couple who gave me tea yesterday. They did not seem to understand, and yet the young husband and father said that he admired what I was doing. I suppose that my job is to sow seeds I may never see grow.

> Do you have joy without a cause,
> Yea, faith without a hope?

So I went down to the breakfast room, the only guest in the stately Grey Lady, and asked the tall young man in a white shirt and black trousers for a large plate of toast and marmalade.

I went out into the morning air £35 lighter, and stood on the bridge over a river to take a photograph of the marina, crowded with yachts and pleasure boats, in a frame of tall willow trees brooding over the still waters of small canals and spacious pools, with the gardens of comfortable homes and cottages running down to their banks.

I crossed the River Trent at the Cavendish Bridge on the A6, and turned down a side road to Castle Donnington. I turned left before reaching the centre of the town and made my way to a village called Hemington. It was fascinating: thatched cottages, village green and medieval parish church standing in a clump of trees. My heart rose and there was a song on my lips. So it was at Lockington, the village which followed. This was truly a glimpse of a vanishing England. Then I left Lockington and moved into the modern madness of a motorway exchange. Only my guardian angel saw me across the heaving, belching concrete of the twisting highway and the road to Kegworth by the A6. In the comparative stillness of a little pub I ordered a meal of salmon sandwiches and a pot of tea.

I bought a newspaper for the first time on the pilgrimage, and found to my incredible joy that Joanna Wilson and her three companions had been declared INNOCENT by that Liverpool jury. If I had a hat I would have thrown it in the air. So I thanked God and Our Lady that justice had been truly done; and despite the delay, I was glad I had been there to help.

Chapter 14

Still Middle England

Before I left the Grey Lady I had booked myself into a B & B at a village called East Leake. I had phoned through to the information centre at Melton Mowbray and they had given me the phone number of several bed and breakfasts, and, although East Leake was less than fifteen miles from Shardlow, I had the gift of an easy day, phoned the East Leake number and had been accepted. I was in no hurry and took time in the pub in Kegworth. There seemed to be no problems. A very minor road crossed the main-line rail track and led to West Leake with its three or four houses, and the stream known as the Kingston Brook; from there would be the last mile-and-a-half to East Leake. And so it proved. I was in East Leake by four in the afternoon, was welcomed by the man of the house, had a wash, made myself a pot of tea in a bedroom, changed into normal clothing, and chatted for some time with mine host.

The house was entitled Sheba, a combination of Sheila and Barry. (Putting the lady's name first and the husband's second, probably because the opposite would have meant calling the house Basher; which would have been unfortunate.) I told him I was walking to Walsingham, and for the first time in this part of the journey, he knew what I meant. He had heard about Walsingham: in fact his wife had been there.

Sheila was a Catholic. She had also been to Medjugorge and Fatima. She was out just at this time, on some business of her own in Kegworth, but she would be in later, and he felt that she would rejoice to hear that I was on a pilgrimage to Walsingham.

68

When the pub down the street opened (they close in all these villages and open at six or seven in the evening, rather as all pubs did before being 'liberated' by the Tory Government), I went for a meal. The food was delicious. By this time I was beginning to find a new kind of appetite. I needed to eat. I needed chicken or fish as well as bread. I knew instinctively that it was not possible to do this journey if I fasted. Fasting was needed at other times. But this was not the time.

Again I noticed the obvious style of the customers. This was Middle England. All those lovely villages had been bought up by men and women who earned high salaries in big towns like Nottingham, and commuted each night to the scented silences of these beautiful English villages. The old cottages standing in clusters around a village green, and a post-card medieval church with a slender spire, had been transformed interiorly by the hard-earned wealth of a new generation. They moved around the carpeted pub with the assured poise of men and women who held securely to a privileged life style. The bar attendants looked like university students paying their way through academic studies. It was all a very different picture from the Kirkby environment, and I felt a stranger in their midst.

There were, however, two old men sitting at a table near me, drinking pints of the local beer, and they dressed and spoke differently to the rest. I guessed that they were genuine locals who had probably come from families who had farmed the land for many generations. I could not understand their accent even though they spoke quite loudly, and I could not help overhearing them.

I went back to my accommodation. Sheila had not yet come in. By 7.45 p.m. I was in bed, recorded the day on my memo taker, and by eight o'clock I was asleep.

I have been reading the diary of the original Cross Pilgrimage of 1948. Maybe I had better explain it.

At the end of the Second World War, the Pope, Pius XII, had called for penance and prayer to heal the gaping wounds of a suffering world. The French had answered by initiating a Cross-bearing Pilgrimage from all quarters of France to a shrine at Vezelay, and an English army officer, Charles Osborne, joined them and was deeply impressed. He therefore

69

conceived the plan for a similar pilgrimage to carry crosses from fourteen different areas of England. Each group was given fourteen days to reach Walsingham with their crosses. They were to meditate each day on the consecutive fourteen Stations of the Cross, each group to consist of twenty or more men. (It was the era of 'men' only). The Liverpool group began from Birkenhead and the journey was one of 220 miles.

It was a tough pilgrimage. The crosses weighed 95 lbs. Three men were to carry the cross in rotation, spells of about ten minutes. Three other men behind the cross were to recite the rosary continually. They were to spend thirteen days on the roads of England. Being a pilgrimage of prayer and penance, school rooms, floors, church halls etc., were to be their resting places and one night was to be spent beneath the stars. England was to witness a public display of prayer, penance and Faith by the Catholic community.

The group from Merseyside met for 8 p.m. Mass in the Church of St Laurence, Birkenhead, were introduced to each other and slept the night on the floor of a school classroom on coconut mats. It was July 2nd, 1948.

The men who took part in this pilgrimage were mostly ex-army. They had lived through one of the most horrendous wars in world history. Rationing was still severe in the England of 1948. Few people had experienced luxurious living. We, all of us (for I was six years ordained already in 1948), were inured to hardship and shortages. So the cross-bearers did not need a big training programme beforehand to get them into shape for the journey.

They used main roads. They did not have the same aversion that drove me away from roads to the moorland footpaths, because traffic in 1948 was minimal compared with the traffic of 1996. They also began from Birkenhead and took a route through Cheshire, avoiding the high lands of the Pennine Chain, moving through Chester, Middlewich, Leek, Ashbourne to Derby and Loughborough. They had gone south in the beginning, where I had chosen to go slightly north to Rochdale and Littleborough. It was to take me sixteen days on the roads: sixteen actual walking days and two days of rest (with the exception of time spent under medical care and the urgency of the court case). The original group had to meet schedules; I did not. They were bound by the need to reach a fixed church hall or schoolroom for the night. I planned that part day by day, being uncertain of how my ancient frame would stand up to the rigours of the road.

But I have many advantages. The boots on my feet are the product of years of research based on the growing popularity of fell walking and mountaineering. I am wearing the Brasher boots. They were probably wearing cast-off army boots, hobnailed things which drove blisters deep into the sole. I have the advantage of modem medical techniques Iike the kind of research which produced the Dr Scholl pads. They had Vaseline and bandages.

I wanted to pray alone and reflect alone. They worked as a group. It was Cistercian versus Carthusian.

What they did was an inspiration for the whole country, and its effects have been lasting. The fourteen crosses stand in a circle now outside the Chapel of Reconciliation at Walsingham where the memories still linger.

But I wanted to make a solitary pilgrimage of thanksgiving to Our Lady and to enter Walsingham unknown and unnoticed to kneel at her feet. (It didn't happen that way !)

Sometimes during these days I dreamt about groups of young men and women following the route I had taken – so much of this wild and beautiful countryside – so that they also could experience something of what I was feeling, of the poetry and wonder of it all. Because this is truly a journey for youth, however you want to define that elusive term. For somewhere in this journey they might see with clearer eyes the futility of things that are, and the deeper things of life. They will see the loneliness and madness of the men and women locked inside the cramped quarters of the cars that swish past relentlessly on the ubiquitous concrete that spills itself all over England like a torrent of lava. They will come away with some kind of vision that they will experience perhaps something

> One instant in a still light
> He saw Our Lady then,
> Her dress was soft as western sky,
> And she was a queen most womanly –
> But she was a queen of men.

71

I have been so fortunate to work with youth groups. Even in Birkdale in wartime, and in the years after the war, I was able to get together a group of young men and a group of young boys. They served at the altar and helped in various projects. Similarly with the girls and young women, using the Legion of Mary. We went for a week's stay in the Lake District, putting up at Ambleside. I was taken on as chaplain to the first secondary modern school in the diocese: it was Our Lady of Lourdes, Birkdale. I learned a great deal about the struggles of young men and women as they grew into maturity. The whole process fascinated me.

Later, in Woolton, I began a youth club which truly blossomed. I was fortunate to have the assistance of young men in the fifth and sixth forms at St Edward's, and the girl's at St Julie's. Every Sunday night we had a crowded and exciting dance session. Although I had a good committee, the most effective discipline was exercised by an old woman, highly respected in Woolton. She stood no nonsense. At this time we booked continuously the fledging Beatles at £7.50 a night. John, Paul, and George trying out new songs and music. The drummer was not Ringo, but some other lad who left them and made room for Ringo. Even at that time their rhythm was truly exciting.

The parish priest was not enthusiastic. He thought their appearance was as bad as their music. He was to change his opinion later when an article in *The Times* prophesied that their music would live. These were heady days. I loved my time in Woolton. Everything was 'swinging'. Liverpool was the place to be, and although the work with youth had its crises and its violence, it was more than worth its headaches.

When I went to Kirkby there was no Catholic youth club in the town, There was an exceedingly good and well run Church of England youth club, Centre 63. There were also youth clubs built and run by the borough, but none came up to the standard of Centre 63.

I think I began a youth club because I needed it more than the youth. All the adults in the parish warned me against it. They had, even at that time, a certain fear of young people. Of course there was violence and vandalism. What could we expect when the birth rate was so high and there were so few facilities for youth?

To begin I put a short notice in the weekly newsletter asking if any young people were interested in scaling mountains or moving over uncharted moorland. If so, meet me at 8 p.m. on a certain Sunday to discuss what we might do. Two young men turned up. They were the first leaders; three months later there were sixty.

We used the Junior School in the beginning. I organized an adult management group, but insisted that the young men and women also had a powerful committee, and that they should have control of some of the funds raised by selling crisps and pop. To control the cash was part of the trust and acceptance of their maturity. The kids wrote their own constitution and controlled the intake of new-comers. Those leaders became very deeply my friends, and I always felt safe on the streets of Kirkby even in the most tumultuous times.

Gradually the original founders left. Many of the boys married the girls. They went to Australia, Canada, and various parts of England. Some remained in the vicinity. They never forgot the youth club and now, thirty years later, they still get in touch with me. And with various ups and downs the youth club has continued throughout thirty years. Now it has changed to 'The Valley YC', and it boasts a purpose-built club leased by the borough to the Catholic Youth Service.

But as I got older I had much less contact with them, My evenings were always so full and it was difficult to fight the extreme fatigue engendered by the life style I had grown into. I do not know what good I did by all this. But God knows and He may have made use of me to touch the lives of some of them and given them a clearer vision of the truth that sets us free. What I do know is that, I never see young men or young girls, no matter how wild and abrasive the boys are, or how brazenly the girl flaunts her sexuality, without feeling a real compassion for them. I wish I could have done more.

73

Chapter 15

Waltham on the Wolds

I phoned through to the information centre at Melton Mowbray and they looked at their accommodation list, no doubt on their computer, and told me that there was B & B available at Waltham on the Wolds.

I took the number and phoned and sure enough there was a room available. Some twenty inches on the map, so with detours and ups and downs it will probably be near to twenty miles. But the weather was fine and the fields were golden with wheat.

There would be a few footpaths, but mostly B roads. At least on a B road I knew where I was going. In Nottinghamshire the footpaths had not been well kept. The stiles were rickety and dangerous. Many of the paths had vanished. In normal circumstances I would not mind that too much. But weighed down by the rucksack and with little energy to spare, it was very hard for me to go a mile down a track and have to turn back because all traces vanished and barbed-wire fences blocked the way. Sometimes this happened because I had misread the map, and I would not like to make false assertions about Nottinghamshire farmers . . . especially on a pilgrimage

Later this day, when I reached Leicestershire, it was very different. The stiles were new, there were waymarks, and the paths really existed. But even with this, the undergrowth was high everywhere and some of the stiles were hidden beneath voracious nettle bushes looking for a patch of bare skin.

So I got lost between Wysal and Willoughby-on-the-Wolds (lovely names) and only found the path with the help of a group of campers.

At Upper Broughton on the A606, I stopped for tea and sandwiches at a fairly large pub. There was an annex where I ate in comfort. In the main bar room there was a coach party of senior citizens. (I qualified; but kept away.) There was a lady compère who entertained them while they had drinks. Many of the coach party were old women. The compère was nauseating. She jollied them on . . . 'Come now, girls!' and all kinds of remarks like, 'How many here have toy boys?' They sang the songs of the twenties; there was a pianist playing for them. I found it degrading and insulting. Old age has its decencies. It is an age of wisdom and reflection: an age of satisfaction and gratitude for what life has held and a humorous acceptance of the inevitability of life. It is the antechamber of eternity, and all this pretence that people are not old, and that one has to be young to be happy, is a grave misunderstanding of the outlook on a future of unending love, peace and joy. It is a time to rest from labour, to enjoy the fruits of life.

Youth is so often a time of uncertainty, hiding inadequacy from aggressive peer groups, pretending that everything is fine when it probably is not, wondering what the future holds, trying to cope with a body that asserts its importance all the time. It is not a golden age. I shuddered at the nonsense being talked by the compère with her blond hair and red lips, trying to fool people who knew a lot more about life than she did.

I went out into the bright sunshine with a feeling of relief, and tried to find the path which would save me walking down the A606. It was on the map, and the map said it passed a place called Bleak Hills, but nobody had heard of Bleak Hills, and in the long run I went four miles out of my way before reaching Holwell in the early evening. I sat by the village green in the evening sun and tried to get some water from the pump, the ancient village pump. There was no water. I waited there for someone like the Samaritan woman in St John's Gospel. But no one came. I took a photograph and, like the water, it did not come out.

Then I left Holwell and the A606 and took the farm road to Scalford. Everywhere the wheat fields stretched to the horizon, endless fields golden brown: wheat standing tall and dignified with the blue sky over it, and the sun setting in a paternal red glow in the West. I was saying the Glorious mysteries; it lifted my heart, and looking at the landscape painting of old age by the Divine Artist, I blotted out the picture of the pub with the coach standing outside and the sound of alcoholic laughter floating from inside. Thank God for reality.

So I took the road to Waltham on the Wolds to a house owned and modified by an architect. He showed me to my room, an attic with a sloping ceiling, a bed, a 14-inch television and a teamaker. The steps up to it were steep and narrow. I had a certain amount of difficulty in manipulating it all. There was a shower and toilet downstairs. I washed and went out to one of two pubs in the village: One was Egon Ronay accredited and I chose it. Why I don't know, because all I wanted was soup and bread and ice cream. But I enjoyed it and crawled back to bed and oblivion.

Chapter 16

Waltham to the Blue Cow

The next morning my breakfast was served by the gentleman who had welcomed me the previous evening. He apologetically told me that his wife had left early to go to her business. We had a long conversation. I told him that I was on pilgrimage to Walsingham.

He told me about his career as an architect. He had been involved in creations in the Middle East, China and Malaysia working for a prestigious firm whose name I forget. Not that it is important, for by this time it will have been gobbled up by someone else.

When he reached some time in the late forties of his life the firm considered him dispensable, and he was given some kind of handshake to sweeten the separation. So he had converted property, like the house we were in, and he was in the process of doing the same to others. This gave him a certain independence, but there was a risk attached, and it was not the same as a guaranteed wage.

I began to see a pattern: Marsden: the man had been a building contractor in the South of England; he had left it behind him, and with his wife had set up the farm and bunkhouse just off the Pennine Way. In Millers Dale it was the same story: man and his wife had come from somewhere like Milton Keynes and bought the lovely little cottage in Derbyshire, with the ground floor for guests. East Leake: the woman was working, and the man was looking after the guests. I had not realised before that this was the changing face of Britain. There seemed to me to be three reasons for it. The tendency in industry is to undervalue loyalty, long service and wisdom, which only comes with experience. This leads company directors to get rid of staff approaching fifty, and bring in young replacements. The process leads to a feeling of insecurity through the whole of the working world. The ruthless survive; the others don't. Wisdom is a rare commodity, not easily found. It does not enter into situations of anxiety, created to be casually exploited. It was not wisdom in Britain that led to Whittle being forced to go to America to sell the idea of the jet engine which he had invented and produced in our country. The same is true of Alexander Fleming and others whose genius was lost to Britain because wisdom was in short supply in our leaders. And so the experience and skill of millions of men is disregarded, and they find outlets for it, or go into a state of decline and deep depression and become victims, instead of creators.

The second reason seems to be the massive unemployment in the past twenty years. That was certainly the reason in Kirkby. The young men so often had to stay at home, get the breakfast for the children, see them off to school, do the shopping etc. The wife or partner had gone to work to bring in the money for the home. Women in Kirkby could get work; the men could not. The work was in care homes, shops, cleaning in schools or factories, and clerical work. The average wage was under £3.00 an hour: apparently the wages are the lowest in Europe. The women worked long hours. It was difficult for the children. They need all the love and attention which so often a tired mother could not give and the father sometimes held back. Men in Britain have to be very careful when they handle children, even their own. It is a sick kind of world. In this world the role of the men and women has altered in ways that previous ages would have found incredible. In many ways it has been beneficial, but there are serious drawbacks.

The third reason is the 'emancipation' of women. Often more highly educated than their husband/partner, they find it difficult to live a life tied to a home. There are a sufficient number of machines available to do the chores which once filled up a day. They take up a leadership role based on intelligence, and being the economic provider. I am still a governor of the Community College of Kirkby; with a student figure of 10,000, it is noticeable how many female students have taken advantage of further education provision. Thank God for all that; it can only be good for the women to reach their full potential.

It is a necessary factor for us, when we contemplate the Church of the future. Certainly in Kirkby the great leveller was unemployment. From the end of the sixties, for twenty devastating years, factory after factory closed on the big industrial estate. Kraft, William Harvey, Dickenson's, Pendleton's, Otis, Birds Eye ... the list could go on interminably. The factories had been the big providers, putting cash into the pockets of people who had never had it before. Alas, they moved elsewhere. They were hard years.

Fr Gerry Hughes offered me two weeks at St Beuno's at the beginning of January in the mid-seventies, free, for the unemployed. It was a marvellous gift from the Jesuits. During one of these weeks, I found one of the men with us had been trained by Volkswagen and had been an accomplished fitter. He could assemble engines, knew all the secrets. We set up a group to refurbish the VW Beetle, used the garage at the back of the parish home to begin with. All the young men were on the dole, and they stayed on it for the first months before being trained. Then they obtained a grant to top up their earnings. We obtained premises then, at St Kevin's school, and went into full production. At one time it looked as though we would expand, and provide them with permanent employment. We ran as a co-operative. It ran for two-and-a-half years and paid its way. Then one January no one paid their bills. We had no capital and had to declare bankruptcy. It was a bitter blow, Later our parish council called a public meeting to decide what we could do about unemployment.

It was held in the parish social centre, and was a very crowded meeting. At the end of it, a woman called Dot Quirk, approached me; she was from a very run-down part of Kirkby, entitled Tower Hill, and was looking for accommodation for a burgeoning Unemployed Centre. At that time I had been asked to look after St Laurence's parish as well as St Joseph's, and there was half a vacant infant school available. I approached the diocese, and they agreed on a nominal rent. It was the beginning of one of the creative institutions which arose out of a nearly impossible situation.

79

The John Moore Foundation offered a sum of money to fund an Administrator. We advertised and there were 85 applicants. After short listing, the applicants were interviewed in the Civic Suite, given free of charge for the purpose. A woman, Christine Davidson, was chosen, There were three of us on the interviewing panel, a shop steward from Pendleton's, a rep from the Transport and General Workers' Union, and myself.

It was a long day, but it was worth it. Christine was a woman who dreamed dreams and made them happen. She formed a strong management committee, with two aims:

To provide a centre for welfare rights.
To be an active group campaigning for justice.

These two sectors came together monthly in a meeting which was a model of patient discussion and rational thought. Sometimes tempers ran high, but the group always respected my presence. We grew to trust each other, They saw a stream of applicants for welfare advice, They spent nights on picket lines, campaigned for the miners in the struggle against the Thatcher Government, and collected for their wives and children.

The premises became too small. Once again our diocese listened to my pleas, and rented the vacant Sacred Heart School, again for a pittance. It flourished ... larger Welfare advice facilities (in one week in a crisis period they saw one thousand applicants!). They opened up a drama section and produced their own street theatre. They opened a serious art department, a crèche, a centre for cheap hot meals, and all this time they were actively involved in the battle for social justice. They were branded as militants. It was untrue. I suppose it was my presence that authenticated them with the uncertain public which heard negative reports about them.

From all these experiences I have learnt, from a very deep level, about the longing for justice at the heart of the poor of our country. They taught me so much. Most of them had some kind of Catholic background. They came to me for the baptism of their grandchildren and their children, for their weddings, and I was there when they were ill and needed confession and the anointing of the sick. I was more and more convinced that this was the work of the Holy Spirit and that, if during these crucial decades, there was no gulf between the Catholic Church and the 'working class' all this had something to do with it.

In all this, I must mention, I had the greatest support and sympathy from the two Bishops, Archbishop Worlock and Bishop David Sheppard. Thank God they were there during those days.

Before leaving Waltham on the Wolds, I bought a copy of the *Guardian* to read about the reaction to the verdict on the four women. Clearly there was a big division of opinion in the country. The tabloids blamed Liverpool! Only scousers would have reached such a verdict, they said, and maybe they were right, but to us that is almost a source of pride. The verdict was just. Those who sell arms to men to commit crimes against humanity, are themselves implicated. The sale is evil, Trying to persuade the dealers that this is true is one of the most difficult of tasks, for dealers are rich and powerful and use their muscle ruthlessly. That four fragile women could have taken them on and won is such a gift from the Lord!

I made my way from Waltham on the Wolds along a sunlit pathway to a farm road, It was about six miles to Wymondham via Saxby. As I approached Wymondham I saw the sails of a windmill in the distance. Reaching it, I found it to be a big complex selling art and artifacts. They also had a good café and I leapt inside with my tongue hanging out. They served me tea and scones, and I re-ordered immediately after I finished the first batch. There were some young girls and their granny at a table near me working their way through cream cakes and coffee. I asked one of the workers outside (for this complex is not complete yet) about the disused railway which I had planned to use as a long-distance footpath But he said it had been closed at various points and was not useable. And one of those points was right here at Wymondham. But I did not give up hope.

I commented on my memo taker about the feeling of awe when I say Mass, and it overwhelms me. Like this morning, in the attic bedroom, I was doing all the wrong things, the door was locked, I had no vestments, I was on my own, and yet I had this feeling of the presence of Christ in my room and seeming to fill the whole house. I find the same thing with the rosary ... like yesterday when I was really very tired and I began the rosary, the Glorious mysteries, and I became absorbed in it, forgot fatigue and the noise of the roadway; and time passes so quickly. The whole thing seems to merge with the meditation and the rhythm of the Hail Marys. I have always said the rosary, just five decades in a day, but it is not like this, the birds and the rabbits, the standing corn in the fields, the swish of cars going past, the air in my face, all part of the mystery as I meditate on it. Yesterday it even seemed to give me a fresh injection of strength overtaking the fatigue. I never felt like this before.

I was making for South Witham; and realized that the disused railway was not going to be viable for me. There were trees and bushes growing in the tunnels, there was no footpath sign; I could see the fenced-off section when I gazed on the map, running through the centre of 'the rail track' all the way to Bourne, but I did not bother trying it because I knew I would feel frustrated.

The road was far busier than I had expected, and, being a B road, there was no footpath. I began to notice the courtesy of the big truck drivers. They used to see me and pull into the centre of the road so as not to threaten me. I would raise my hand in salute, and the drivers would give a thumbs-up sign. I welcomed their courtesy.

Not all the private cars were as considerate, but on the whole people were good and did not drive me into the ditch. Needless to say no one else was walking. I was in a world of my own.

And so I came to South Witham, and sat down on a stone by the Blue Cow Inn and waited for Stella.

Chapter 17

Stella and John

Stella and John live at Stamford, Lincs, which is a comparatively short car journey from my route. I had been introduced by Stella's sister Doreen, not face to face, but by telephone, so when she came in the car, I would not know her. But she would know me, partly because I had phoned her to say I was by the Blue Cow (and most people never yet had sat by a blue cow): but also because I was walking and had a rucksack to prove it. As I have mentioned, no one walks south-east of Derbyshire.

So there was no doubt that she would find me. Her sister Doreen who effected the introduction was a long-standing friend of mine. She had resigned her nursing post some years before, having uniquely reached the position of deputy Matron of the Royal Liverpool Infirmary.

In its heyday this had been one of the great hospitals, a large Victorian building with spacious corridors lined with white tiles. The wards in the hospital were long dormitories with each bed and its coverlet the correct statutory distance from the beds on each side. The regime was statutory, also very martial. The ward sister was a formidable figure, ensuring good timekeeping by the nurses, all of whom had to be correctly dressed in spotless uniforms. Visits by relatives were restricted, and all this was also strictly enforced. Each morning the Matron came round to inspect and admonish. At least once a day, divinity in the shape of a consultant moved down the ward in an awed silence, except for whispers from white-coated doctors, dripping with stethoscopes.

It was liturgy, semi-religious, giving a deep feeling about the omnipotence of science, and the care and devotion of its

83

priesthood. It may also have been better for patients' care than the melée in the crowded wards of modern hospitals in a different era.

But, anyway, back to Doreen; she was a Catholic in a high position in the nursing hierarchy and that was something unusual at that time. Many of the nurses were Welsh, for Liverpool is near the Welsh borders. They were good girls, hard-working and trustworthy.

Their religion was normally the one they had imbibed in the Bible classes and the little chapels of the valleys and hills of their native land. In the century and a half which followed the reformation and the dismembering of the Catholic Church, the people of Wales had been very much left to their own devices. They were (and are) of a different culture, with a distinctive Celtic language, isolated by high mountains and deep wide wooded valleys.

It took the followers of the great John Wesley to evangelize them. The result was a native religion of white goodness and badness, severe as the mountains and as uncompromising as the harsh slate quarries. But with it went a great love for their communities and a solidarity of heart and mind, and they sang the great Wesley hymns with a passion and beauty unrivalled in the British Isles.

But they carried with them also a deep suspicion of the Catholic Church, as the Catholic school teachers found in the 1940s when they took care of the children who were evacuated from wartime Liverpool to the heart of pastoral Wales.

Hence for a Catholic to become deputy Matron of the Royal was unusual.

It was similar, but not quite as bad as the prevailing case of gynaecology, in which practising Catholics had no chance of promotion, and probably no chance of a job. It is a savage case of religious discrimination as bad as anything which existed before the Act of Catholic Emancipation of 1825; except that in this case it is based on *abortion* and not on an Act of Uniformity. So the field is left clear for men like Dr. B. who performed an abortion on a wealthy lady due to have twins, who really only wanted one baby, then left it to a consultant to determine which baby would die. Millions saw his face peering from the front page of the *Daily Express* dressed in his surgical costume looking like a mobile gas chamber. He explained that he tore the baby limb from limb to extricate the victim from the womb! 'Gynaecology'! He said, 'Yes, I do more abortions than deliveries.'

The car drew up in front of the Blue Cow, and Stella got out and introduced herself; we drove the fifteen miles to the Old Bakehouse. Stella had retired from teaching some years before: John, her husband, likewise. He had retired from business and was now interested in politics. He had been elected as the Labour representative of his ward in the latest round of municipal elections. At the time when I arrived he was in London on business. Stella and John have fallen in love with Stamford, and when some time later I was able to walk its streets, I understood why. There is a Catholic Church near their home, with a flourishing and active congregation. That night I enjoyed an omelette, a hot bath and a very comfortable bed.

On the first morning of my stay in the house of Stella and John, I said Mass for the first time since Glossop, in the downstairs lounge, with Stella sharing Mass. Once more I was overwhelmed by the sense of the presence of Jesus. It was Friday morning; the Mass is so truly a sacrifice; the separation of the white host and the red wine before my eyes. I get so conscious of a white body on a cross against the black sky, and the red blood on the ground beneath ... all these emotions, and the presence of Stella praying for her son who was going on a long journey for something which eluded him.

Then she drove me back to South Witham, and I moved on a footpath to Morkey Wood and along another footpath to Castle Bytham. I was looking for a footpath along the railway. The road followed faithfully, like a dog after a bone. The disused railway began to be an obsession with me. It was there but it was not possible to walk it. Just after a hamlet called Little Bytham, the map showed it now becoming a roadway, not just a path, so I decided to have a go at it. I went down a side farm road to reach it and ran in to a big gate with a large notice saying PRIVATE. I took a photograph of the notice and sat down and opened a flask of tea. There was a dog barking on my left. I decided that I would not risk it: dark and evil thoughts were running through my head and I had to talk to myself. 'Listen, YOU, this is a pilgrimage, not a crusade to open footpaths.'

Leaving this farm track, still occupied with the battle within. I stopped a car which was making for the track towards the barred gate marked Private. The car stopped and I asked the young man driving it about the reason for the closure of the pathway. He was surprised: 'Yes,' he said, 'the path is there, I have walked on it often.'

He pondered on the closure. He suggested that he had had access to it because he lived and worked on 'the estate'. (So somebody had bought the land.) He suggested that possibly there was a shooting party and they needed to close it off for safety.

He was a nice young man and obviously trying to be helpful. So I took the detour to Witham on the Hill thinking about the many voiceless people who lose their rights to the rich and powerful, and have no way of recovering their rights; unfortunately the world is full of them. In so many parts of the world they know they are powerless, and live and die angry.

It was one of the great gifts that we had the Unemployed Centre in Kirkby to champion the rights of the poor. At one time there was a major drive to find people who were using the services of the DHSS and earning illegally by taking jobs in pubs and clubs. It was a necessary project, because there are those who do this and threaten the very existence of national help for the poor. But the system chosen was to send undercover people to mingle with the people who use the pubs and clubs, and they became known as 'Snoopers'. By means known only to the Centre, the activists discovered the number plates of the snoopers' cars and published the numbers in the area, making life difficult for the agents. But it was action of this kind which gave the Centre the reputation of being militant. This did not help, during one by-election due to the death of Sean Hughes who was MP for South Knowsley. The Social Democrats had a strong candidate, Rosie Cooper. She mounted a campaign against the Centre as part of her appeal to the voters. She asked permission to canvass St Joseph's Social Club, and I agreed that she should. I also asked her to call and see me, which she did later in the evening, accompanied by a powerful entourage, including Shirley Williams and

David Alton. I made them welcome and made them coffee and refreshments. Rosie was a good woman, full of enthusiasm. She began to talk about 'The Militants' in the Unemployed Centre. I stopped her. 'Rosie,' I said, 'I personally appointed many of these people, and you are making a mistake.' They asked me a lot of questions then. From that time on, she did not use this denunciation of the Unemployed Centre as part of her campaign.

This distraction was a gift. I am not in that world now. I'm on a pilgrimage of love and thanks to the Mother of God. It is the better part, it will not be taken from me. I recognized a phenomenon which I have met again and again in any good work I have been engaged in. At some point the angel of darkness makes his presence felt, side tracking the mind and leading to a loss of inner peace In the same way, if I am planning and praying for a spiritual campaign along with a group, the evil one enters in and tries to cause confusion and division.

It was after the detour to Witham on the Hill that I found a footpath which led me, to my immense surprise, to the very rail pathway which for so long had eluded me. It led me to a submerged path under tunnels and among brier bushes and nettles to a farm path straight into the centre of Bourne, and as I walked into it, I saw Stella pulling into a side street. It was four o'clock and that was the time we had arranged to meet. I thanked the good guardian angel that had seen me through that curious temptation.

I had already decided that the next day, Saturday, I would have a day of rest and it was delightful to relax in the comfort of the Old Bakehouse.

Chapter 18

Day of Rest

This was the Saturday when I rested at the Old Bakehouse. I sat out in the small garden at the back of the house enjoying the luxury of reading and dozing. I had taken only one book with me on the journey. In addition to the small New Testament I used in the place of the breviary, it was *Aquinas* by F.C. Copleston. It was a strange choice. It's not easy reading, but it fitted my thinking, and because of the seminary background the concepts of the book were familiar.

Aquinas was indeed a genius. He was born in Italy about the year 1225, spent part of his childhood at Monte Cassino, the famous monastery founded by St Benedict and destroyed by the Allied Forces in 1944. (It has since been rebuilt with American dollars.) He was barely fifteen when he went to study at the University of Naples. He entered the newly-founded Dominican Order, an order of mendicant friars on the pattern of the Franciscans; this choice was anathema to his aristocratic family. They would not have minded if he had become a respectable canon or bishop . . . but a friar! They were like the flower people of the sixties; his family was shocked. They locked him a tower in their castle and, the story goes, they put a prostitute into the room in the hope that she would seduce him. But he chased her out of the cell with a burning stick from the fire on the hearth of the room. She didn't go back.

He went to the University at Paris and studied under Albert the Great. He became a teacher there and was ordained to the priesthood, spent some time at the University of Cologne and was recalled to Paris to take the chair of Theology in 1256.

He used the writings of the ancient Greek philosopher Aristotle, newly introduced into Europe by the Arabian philosophers Averroës and Avicenna, who had arrived in Spain with the all-conquering Muslims – the same group which had overrun Alexandria and opened up Greek thought. Because of this contact with the dreaded Muslims, Aquinas was interrogated by the Inquisition and was for a long period suspected of heresy. His output was phenomenal. His great works the *Summa Theologica* and *Contra Gentiles* would take a lifetime to read, but they were only part of his output. He died when he was forty-nine, and for more than seven hundred years his lucid thought dominated the theology of the Catholic Church.

I came across him when I was following the standard philosophy course which was mandatory at that time for students for the priesthood. It was a period in my life when I was searching for stability and certainty. I wanted to be a priest. I knew it involved total commitment, ruling out married love and other attachments. I was prepared for that. But I needed to know that the basis of faith was reasonable. I was immature, and did not want to give my life for something which was beyond my power to defend with rational thought. Now I know that the whole concept of the abasement of Christ and his horrible death was totally irrational in normal terms and that the resurrection was not something anyone could have worked out by common sense. But I had not reached that stage by the time I was eighteen.

I had spent months during my adolescence suffering from a strange psychological illness. I had come face to face with the poverty of the thirties, read the newspapers, like the Beaverbook press which idolized the triumphs of Mussolini and the startling successes of Adolf Hitler, the new German Messiah solving problems of unemployment, by building massive roads, promising a new life to everyone, and beginning the legend of the *wandervogel* – the young men and maidens with guitars and rucksacks in the youth camps of the Black Forest. It all looked so good. I read *Mein Kampf* and was impressed, but became uncertain of so much that had previously seemed so rock-solid.

It was at that time in my life that I found St Thomas

Aquinas. I read him in Latin because the language suited his thought: anyhow, our lectures were in Latin. I was thrilled in a way nothing had ever thrilled me. I began to eat less food because my mind was clearer when I was hungry. The heating in the college was inadequate, but I could forget cold and hunger and become immersed in this incredible mediaeval writer.

I would not open letters from home until late in the afternoon in case they distracted me. Never in my short life as a student had I met anything as lucid as this. At various times in my life I have re-read parts of the *Summa Theologica*. As late as last year when I was asked to give a talk, advertized in Knowsley Community College under the title 'God Does Exist', I read again the Five Ways in the Latin version.

Now, at this stage in my life, I know that they are not adequate, and he – St Thomas – never intended them to stand on their own, but they still thrilled me by the sheer crisp logic of his statements with every word in place; not a single adjective, not a single emotive idea. Thought – washed in dazzling whiteness and wrung dry in the wind of the spirit, challenging over several hundred years the unreason of the poor atheist. So I read again in my old age, knowing that it does not prove the existence of God, except for the believer, and remembering how I said as a youth, 'That will do for me'.

I put him in my small gallery of saints I trust and fell in love with: in the same shrine in my heart as the Blessed Virgin, St Theresa of Liseux, and as the years passed I added St Patrick, because of Lough Derg, and St Francis of Assisi, because I saw the poverty in the people I lived with; and St Bernadette, because like me she was tiny and inadequate, and yet she was used by God and Our Lady to produce something extraordinary.

So I sat for part of the day in the garden of the Old Bakehouse. It was also the day that John came home from London, and the day I went with Stella to see the elegance of Stamford, Lincs, and joined the Catholic people who attended the evening Mass in the church, the first Mass of Sunday.

At the end of the Mass I met the priest, Fr Laurence Saunders, standing in the evening air outside the lovely church of St Mary and St Augustine, built in the middle of the nineteenth century, just after the restoration of the hierarchy in England and the end of the long night of the Reformation. I wondered how it was that a group of Catholics had been found at that time, in this part of Central England, to build a church as sound and as attractive as this.

It was not the time to ask Fr Laurence these questions. It had been a memorable day and a rest was probably overdue. So we celebrated Mass together next morning, John, Stella and I.

The rucksack was packed, I took a photograph, which did turn out; it showed John and Stella side by side at the front door of the Old Bakehouse. Stella then drove me to Bourne, to the place where I had met her on Friday evening. I said Goodbye and Thank you, and turned in the direction of Spalding.

Chapter 19

The Fen Country

The Fen country begins at Bourne. Flat, criss-crossed with canals and large ditches – it stretches for miles to the sea.

Stella and John and the dog drove me to Bourne, and we said good-bye. It had been a golden two days and had put me on my feet again, and begun a friendship which I hope will continue. I saw the car vanish down the road. I was in a quiet part of what is a quiet town, and it was Sunday morning; and Sunday morning is a quiet morning, so all around was a big hush. I had spent time with the map and knew what I wanted – not the main road to Spalding, but a B or a C road which on the map runs alongside one of the broad canals. It was clearly marked on the map.

But since the map had been published, a new housing estate had been built and a new industrial estate. I now wandered through the housing estate, then the industrial estate, looking for the path alongside the canal. I met one man – but he was a man with a map as well and he was as lost as I, except that he was heading in the opposite direction. So I sat on a low wall, took out the map and the compass and very carefully took a bearing. Then I walked along the deserted streets and suddenly I saw it: South Fen Road.

It ran absolutely straight for miles. Scarcely a car or a tractor roamed its surface. The sun had come out, and climbed steadily into an azure-blue sky. A wind blew into my face and I opened my nose and my lungs to its smell of reeds and ditches and the purity of its inhalation.

The sky was amazing. It seemed to reach down to the horizon like it was shaking hands with it. White clouds sailed across like jet trails. I skipped along and the whole thing became part of the five Joyful mysteries of the rosary.

I reached a T-junction at a wider road and turned left – east, in the direction of Spalding.

This road was busier and not as pleasant, but I knew that it was right and there was no other. This is one of the things about this part of the country; there are no obvious footpaths; they do exist but they link farmhouses across fields and go nowhere else, so there is no point in using them. In fact the road that I was walking was a country road and I knew where I was going, so I was happy.

Some two miles from Spalding I sat on a grassy bank near a pub at the first crossroads, ate a sandwich and drank a flask of tea. A girl drove up in an L registered Fiesta and asked where the fishing pond was. I looked up the map and told her: I felt very professional. It's funny how you get proud over daft things like that; but then I think I impressed her, and it's not often that happens.

I went to Spalding. It was midday and the heat was stifling. I pulled the white hat with a broad brim out of the rucksack and put it on to save myself from sunstroke, and so apparelled I went into a pub at the corner of three streets. It was an old pub, and looked in need of a coat of paint. Inside was no different. No brewery had bothered to spend money on it; no carpets here. Lino, brown lino, as it should be in a pub like this. As my friends used to say in Kirkby – it had 'atmosphere'. There was a cat sitting on a stool near the bar gazing Buddha-like across the room, and it never stirred the whole time I was in. I thought of the old ballad which began 'There's a green-eyed yellow idol to the north of Katmandu'. The green eyes of the cat never flickered and the fur rose gently with its breathing, as though it was a case of passive intoxication.

There were eight men gathered round a laden table of bottles and glasses. They were not dressed in their Sunday best, but it was very clear that this was their territory; and I imagine that Sunday after Sunday they met there until three o'clock, then went home to the 'roasties' and beef and sprouts. There was dead silence when I walked in, in my hat and rucksack and dusty boots. I ordered a glass of lemonade

93

and blackcurrant from a round-faced girl with lipstick and blonde hair. 'Please, with ice.'

Then one of the men spoke. He was an old man: he had a pint inside him, and he said, 'He's like a desert Rat.' That dated him. I laughed and laughed, because he was partly right. I was burnt brown with the sun and wind, my ugly face was thin and lined, and I was in big boots and carrying a pack. He was wrong about the war zone. I looked more like a stray from *The Bridge over the River Kwai*. As I laughed they relaxed and asked me where I was going. 'I'm going to Walsingham in Norfolk,' I said.

They said, 'What are you going for?'

I answered, 'Its a kind of pilgrimage.'

Silence again – I was not sure that they understood what that meant.

'Where are you from?'

'Liverpool.'

'I don't blame you for getting out of there, mate.'

Then the old man who had spoken first said, 'Get him a pint.'

'No, no,' I said hastily, my mind flashing back to the time in the Pyrenees when I went into a bar to get water to make tea, and had been forced to toast Winston Churchill in Pernod. 'I have enough here, but thanks a lot, mate.'

The old man looked at me again. 'How old are you?' he said.

I said, 'I'm seventy-eight.'

They took time to digest this, and I finished the lemonade and blackcurrant. Then one of the men stretched out his hand: 'You're fantastic,' he said.

Then I had to shake all their hands, one after the other, picked up my rucksack and went out into the sunlight.

I understood men like that, there is something special about them.

So I took the road to Weston on the A151. I reached it soon after 4 p.m. My destination was a bungalow, in a group of houses and flats for the elderly and infirm, able to summon help from a resident warden at the push of a red button or the pull of a red cord. In one of these bungalows lived my hostess for the night. She was a retired priest's housekeeper; now a widow, she was recommended by the S.V.P. Stella had phoned to tell her about me. She had said, 'Yes, please.' She was waiting for me at the door and made me very welcome.

She had lived some fifteen years in the presbytery, with her husband Jim, and taken care of the priest in a busy parish in the south. She had loved the work. Jim, her husband, had continued working until his retirement, when he gave his skills and dedication to looking after many of the little jobs that needed doing in the presbytery and church. The priest eventually had some trouble which led the Bishop to send him away for psychological treatment. At that point they left his service.

They decided on taking a bungalow in this settlement because she was born in the Spalding area and was happy to return to it. At that time they qualified for a place in a new secure housing unit because of their age. Soon after moving in, Jim, her husband, had died leaving her life blank. She loved him deeply and found the loneliness hard. The bedroom she had allocated me was the bedroom which she had shared with him. After his death she was unable to return to it, and made a small room opposite into her own bedroom.

She made me an omelette because there was no pub to which I could go for a meal, and we sat talking late into the night.

The next morning I said Mass for Jim and she joined in a very emotional Mass. She also gave me a small book with the Morning and Evening Prayer of the church, and from that time onwards I used it instead of the New Testament and Psalms which had been used in so many exciting places by Tom Mckenna.

I left Vicarage Lane early on Monday morning. Before I left I took a photograph of this gracious lady standing in her garden, and it is before me now as I write.

Chapter 20

The Road to King's Lynn

I took the A151. There seemed no alternative; this was the fen country, and it was not kind to long-distance footpaths. Also, there was a pavement, and that meant that I could concentrate on my own thoughts and not spend time avoiding the traffic. Thoughts I had a-plenty.

Firstly, I had to make my mind up about shelter for the night. It was some twenty-four miles to King's Lynn, and I had been warned not to do that kind of distance on the roads. It would be different if there were footpaths. There is a motel at Long Sutton, Trusthouse Forte: thirty-five pounds a night for the room, but luxurious. That did not attract me; it would be a distraction. So I decided to keep on walking and see how things went: not the advice I would give anyone; it was a result of indecision.

The second object of my thoughts was less mundane. It concerned a young man Stella had talked about, whom I had not met. She described him as highly intelligent and very spiritual. He had taken indefinite leave from whatever profession he followed to go to India, in search of more stimulating spirituality than that which he had found in the western world. He had been brought up a Catholic, but did not find it satisfying. He had decided to go and sit at the feet of an Indian mystic, on the advice of his friend who recommended a certain person to him.

I had met this thinking before and it disturbed me; and at this time of my life I feel totally certain that any advanced spirituality is already present in the tradition and practice of the Catholic Church, but that it lies undiscovered.

I had been brought up in childhood in the tradition of my parents. That involved the Mass every Sunday, and when I became a server, serving Mass every weekday as well. I had been taught certain prayers to say at night and in the morning; to receive Holy Communion and go to Confession when my mother thought I should. I never questioned this. It was the atmosphere of the home. My father and mother lived it, and life centred around the major feasts of the Church and the liturgical seasons such as Christmas, Lent and Easter and so on. Unconsciously I was absorbing a great deal of joy: colour, mystery, poetry, art, and a sense of joy especially. Religion was not forced on us in the family. It was as fundamental as Christmas pudding, Bob-apple night, and rice pudding on Sunday.

I went to the seminary at the age of eleven, and absorbed retreats, Latin liturgy, the *schola puerorum* and the intricacies and plaintive melodies of Gregorian chant. Christmas Midnight Mass in the seminary was wonderful, as was the music of Holy Week, litanies etc, and after the first years we were introduced to 'Meditation' – half an hour each morning. Meditation was based on Jesuit thinking. Retreats were almost always given by Jesuits. The preparation for the morning meditation was based on Ignatian methods. It was a discipline, a mental routine rather than a prayer: I found it arid, soul-destroying. A gospel; three points (it was always three); consider this, consider that. Put yourself into it. What would you say to Him when you were inserted into the incident at page X in the Gospel? This was to lead to a few random prayers which were genuine. Then more scaffolding, wind it up, check it out. Look at it again at night and get ready for the next morning – it was not for me. I know this sounds very naughty; and I very deeply admire the Jesuits and St Ignatius their founder.

The mistake made in the seminary was that we were not given any real alternative, and I do not think the professors took a deep enough interest in it. I only remember one retreat in the whole thirteen years, and that was given by a Benedictine, Dom Graff. He fascinated me and I remember the phrase of St Benedict, *'Solus cum Solo'*, in the cave at Subiaco, and it haunted my mind.

I was to discover more about that later. My favourite saint

for the early years was Thérèse of Liseux. Her Little Way also fascinated me. But it was years afterwards, after flirting with the thought of joining the Cistercians (the Abbot said 'No, your place is with the people') that I was handed a copy of the works of St John of the Cross by Edward Stephens, the parish priest I served under in Birkdale, and I found what I was searching for.

I read *The Ascent of Mount Carmel*, *The Dark Night of the Soul*, and *The Living Flame of Love*, through the course of one intense year, and stepped out of Ignatian spirituality. I think we were just given it the wrong way. I think that something like that must have happened to the lad who went to India to look for help.

But, for me, it was a sinking into the darkness of God. In the tumultuous years in Kirkby, I needed that hour early every morning. It became more important than food and drink. I said it was my 'fix', like the kids on drugs.

My mother, when I was a young priest, had given me a heavy cloak, and I used to wear it wrapped around me in the cold and darkness of the winter mornings in the church when there was no light except the sanctuary lamp flickering near the tabernacle, and the sound of milkmen and the early buses. It seemed such a shame that someone had to go to India when it was all waiting on the doorstep: one of the best-kept secrets of the Church of Silence.

One of my idiosyncrasies is that the deeper my thoughts, the faster I walk, and by eleven o'clock I found myself at Holbeach. The heat was stifling. There was not a breath of wind and the sun was high in the August sky. I bought an ice-cold drink and stopped outside the shop to drink it. I would have liked a pot of tea but could not see a café or coffee shop anywhere.

There were two Indian takeaways and one Chinese in the street. I don't believe they are all genuine immigrants anyway: one of the taxi drivers in Kirkby became disenchanted with running the taxi business. He was a scouse of the scousers and opened a takeaway under the title 'Charlie Wong'. He said he was just 'managing' the shop from Shanghai. But the only time he had left the Liverpool docks was to see Liverpool FC playing Juventus.

On the other side of the road to the shop selling cold drinks was a beautiful medieval church. Now Anglican, it was built two hundred years before the Reformation and with all the love and care of master stonemasons and builders. There must have been deep and dynamic Faith in the hearts of the Catholics of those centuries who raised these jewels of religious architecture and bequeathed them to the unborn ages, so often, as now, unworthy of the special bequest.

The church was open, and I took shelter from the heat in the cool, shadowy interior. The Gothic roof soaring up into the dimness, the round pillars half-Norman, half-Gothic, bearing testimony to the long years before the building reached its present perfection; the all-pervading sense that the stone walls were permeated with the prayers of thousands of men and women who had found Faith in here and had gone to God 'shriven and annealed' and fortified with the Viaticum.

In one corner there was a tomb surmounted by the stone figure of a knight in full armour, and by his side the stone carving of someone's severed head. I took a photograph, and looking at it, it is difficult to say whether it is male or female. The knight has his hands joined as though in prayer. It is a curious piece of sculpture. It seemed to be the custom to adorn tombs in this way. The man had to be in armour and have a sword, as though this made him real. To me it seems such warped thinking. The last thing you look for in the dedicated Christian is dressing him up like a warrior, a guy who kills people, the macho man. Like the appearances of Sadam Hussein, always in battledress; goes to bed in it!

Colonel Gadaffi puts on the act as well, Stalin had a go at it: Uncle Joe, the brave fighter. But it is certainly not Christian. It is possible that it was a remnant of the Crusades when the knights rode out to save the Christian Holy Land from the Saracens and built battlements and towers in Malta, Crete, and Sicily to hold back the all-conquering armies of Suliman the Magnificent. But I doubt if the stone knights dotted around the tombs of Britain all fell within this category.

I picked up my rucksack and went out into the sunshine and took the road to Fleet Hargate and the meeting with the dreaded A17.

The A17 is the main road from the A1 to King's Lynn for

those coming from the north. For most of its miles it is just a single carriageway which carries heavy traffic to and from Norfolk. It is not pleasant driving on it. It is a nightmare walking on it, so at Fleet Hargate I took a minor road on the right which added nearly a mile extra, but meant that I could cross the A17 at Gedney and join the B road leading to Long Sutton.

I reached Long Sutton at 1.30 p.m. This was the place near the Forte motel, and I knew then that I would not stay the afternoon and night in a motel while the sun was shining and the day was still young. So I moved out of Long Sutton and took the B Road to Sutton. I was carrying a turkey sandwich and a piece of home-made cake wrapped up for me by the lady in sheltered accommodation. She put all that together and did not want any payment for the food and the night's lodgings, but she was poor and I would not hear of it. She had little boxes in the bedroom marked 'telephone', 'gas' and 'water'.

That was the method chosen by the pensioners in Kirkby so that they could put a bit away from their pension each week to meet bills when they came in. I persuaded her to take the cost of the night and the food. The sandwich and cake were delicious.

There was a pavement on the road to Sutton Bridge, and I was able to ignore the traffic and say the rosary and become immersed in my thoughts. The wind was blowing in my face, and I was dyed dark brown by the wind and the sun. As the big trucks passed by they created a dust storm, and I had to hold my hat down in case it blew away, like the little red woolly one lost on Soldier's Lump. But apart from this I found that I could shut myself off from the endless noise of the traffic and felt safe on the pavement; by five o'clock I was at Sutton Bridge, and called into a pub for my usual pint of iced lemonade and blackcurrant.

The group of drinkers once again asked me questions, and warned me to ignore the A17 (as though I didn't know) and take the old A17 which went through Walpole and Terrington St Clement. One of them took me to the door of the pub and went to his car. He motioned me inside and ran me to the beginning of the old A17, a distance of about half a mile.

All the way on this pilgrimage I had met with kindness and

consideration from these ordinary men. I took this tree-lined road as the evening drew on. I was entering a part of England which had created an economic miracle in medieval times. It was a vast expanse of country, growing flax and rearing sheep. In all these areas from little ports situated along the canals, flat-bottomed boats had sailed to the continent with wool and cotton dyes.

The merchants had become very rich; it was seen in the numerous churches with chantries erected for priests to offer Masses for the souls of the benefactors. The parishes had the name of Saints like Terrington St Clement and Terrington St James. The churches had tall spires, very slender in white stone, seen for miles over the flat countryside, and very photogenic.

So I crossed the Great Ouse river some five miles beyond Terrington St Clement, by a road to King's Lynn.

I was getting tired by now and made an error in judgement in doing this, so that the final mile was by a high embankment footpath on the opposite side of the river. I felt very elated. I knew now that, barring an accident, nothing could stop me from reaching Walsingham. The dream was becoming reality.

There lives in King's Lynn a Canadian named Frank Prouse. He had seen the advert for the first cross-bearing pilgrimage at the end of the war, and joined it at Glossop in Derbyshire, Fifty year later, when Monsignor John Furnival asked for volunteers, for the fiftieth anniversary of the epic journey, Frank had answered and joined once more. On that second journey he had spent a night with John and Stella, and they had phoned him to meet me at King's Lynn. He had not been free to do this, but had arranged that a certain Terry Martin would stand in for him. At the time I had planned to reach King's Lynn on Tuesday, and the meeting point was to be the church of Our Lady in London Road. So, after crossing the bridge across the river; I found my way to London Road and to the church of Our Lady.

101

Chapter 21

King's Lynn

Because I was a day earlier than I had planned, it was clear that there would be no one to meet me, so I conjectured that the priests at the parish house of Our Lady of the Annunciation, in London Road, would welcome me into their home, allow me to telephone Frank to explain that I was twenty-four hours too early, and, while I waited for something to happen, hospitable Fathers would provide me with a big pot of tea and a plate of toast, which at that moment I needed quite badly.

The church stood prominently in view, only separated from London Road by a railing of wrought iron and a strip of grass. It looked from the outside to be a well-built traditional type of church. I discovered later that the first church had been built in 1778, and that this present one had been an enlargement, almost a rebuilding, in 1987. So clearly there was a substantial Catholic presence in King's Lynn over two centuries. I might have expected this because of the connection of King's Lynn with continental trade. I tried the door of the church to see if I could peep in but it was locked. With a vision of tea, toast and jam almost ballooning out of my head à la cartoon, I tried to find the presbytery. It was not easily visible.

There was a small passageway running alongside the church with houses built each side of it. I went to the nearest house and knocked. A young mother answered, with a child tugging at her skirts. 'I beg your pardon,' I began politely, realizing that I still looked like a desert rat, 'do you know the house where the priest lives?' (That sounds very complicated but I guessed that she would not be a Catholic.) She seemed to ponder the question. She said, 'I'm sorry, I don't know.' She closed the door. Just then a young man riding a bicycle came down the close. I asked him the question. 'It's that house there,' he said, pointing to a door at the top of a flight of steps.

It was almost precisely next door to the lady with the child, but squeezed in at the top of the steps and almost invisible. I thought later that the lady may have known, guessed that I might be looking for a handout, which I was, and didn't want the priest troubled by ageing desert rats. That would be at least worth a plenary indulgence.

I climbed the steps and rang the bell: no reply!

I rang again one, twice, three times. No one answered, not even a dog barking. This was Horwich again. I did not say any bad words because I was on pilgrimage. By this time exhaustion had really gripped me. I walked almost unsteadily down the long street looking for a phone box. Then I phoned Frank Prouse's number, and mercifully he was in. Half an hour later he handed me over to the care of Josie and Henry Warner. They had only half an hour to prepare for me, but the welcome was genuine. I knew I was at home,

That night I sat up late, talking with Josie. In between eating sandwiches and drinking pots of tea, she told me her life story. It was one of the phenomena I had noticed on the journey; so many wanted to open their hearts to me, a complete stranger, knowing full well, and correctly, that what they told me would remain a secret. I suppose over the fifty-four years of being a priest I had unconsciously developed the gift of listening and the gift of compassion. This had grown with me to such a depth that with people thronging all around me, I can listen to a man or a woman talking to me and become oblivious to all the crowd around me, and listen only to the whispered voice of someone who is in need.

Pictures will form in my mind; names of people will become real and situations are etched on my imagination as though I was watching a film unrolling to its end. It will stay with me deep in my conscious thought, and then or next morning in the hour with the Master I will talk to Him about it. I am more and more aware of the truth of the words of Jesus: 'Whatever you ask my Father in my Name He will give to you. Whoever asks will receive; to whomsoever knocks, the door will be opened.' Now I know it is true. I believe it, not with my head but with my heart.

Time after time people come back to me or write to me and say 'Thank you, thank you; the situation has changed.' And then I thank God who loves his children. I now know that it is true, that prayer is all-powerful. I confess that when I was young I did not believe it. I said I did, but I did not. I would consciously say 'If God wants it', which meant . . . IF . . . and that hesitation betrayed my unbelief. So I would only too readily say 'Yes' when people asked me to pray for something, and then I would forget it. I knew I should not forget, so I would make a general intention during Mass at the part of the Eucharistic prayer where we pray for the needs of our brothers and sisters, just a nod in the direction of someone I had already forgotten, and I was doing it to satisfy my conscience about a promise made lightly. But I don't do that now. The voices of those in need are too important, and I get this sensation of time standing still while a voice talks to me about some deep human need which I have to pass on to the Lover.

Josie had come from Ireland at the beginning of the war and met Henry in the munitions factory where they both worked. He was a young technician and he loved her. He embraced her Faith and married her, and now she and the faith she had carried with her from Ireland was part of his life.

The next morning Frank arrived at the back of the house at eight o'clock, and other friends from around about came in and filled the room. There I celebrated Mass and offered it for Josie and Henry. The whole house was full of peace and a sense of joy that was almost tangible.

Then there were lashings of tea and coffee and rounds of toast and the kind of talk which happens when people are spiritually at one with each other. They drifted out as they had drifted in. One of the men offered to transport my rucksack in his car to my next night's lodging. Frank said he would come back with a little knapsack to carry my waterproofs and sandwiches. We also discussed whether I should walk the twenty miles to Walsingham or break the journey.

He also told me that the New Dawn Conference was on, and

that the shrine might be very crowded. I asked him how many people would be at the New Dawn and he said at least two thousand. I had not booked up to now, and there might be nowhere for me to stay. In that case it would be folly to arrive there late in the evening and begin looking for digs. I would need to be there by midday to have a chance of getting anything. Nor would there be any sense in phoning ahead, because they would just say, 'There is no room here; come back next year'.

So I searched the map, saw a village called Great Bircham and there was an inn. I phoned the information centre at King's Lynn. They told me that the inn offered accommodation, and gave me the phone number. I rang and they said yes, there was a single room available. I settled for that and booked it.

Frank went home for the knapsack and I began my preparation for the last part of the journey.

It was a sunny day. My friend came for the rucksack; Frank turned up with the ancient knapsack which, he said, had already journeyed twice down that road. Outside the house I took a photograph; the tall wiry Canadian, Henry smiling, but a little stooped now, and between them, Josie from Ireland looking as bright as a hillside meadow in Donegal touched by the morning sun.

Chapter 22

Norfolk

I took the A148 towards Fakenham, a little worried by the prospect of meeting the New Dawn Conference. The New Dawn is a meeting of charismatics, and I am not attuned to the charismatic movement. In the Catholic Church before the Second Vatican Council, there were movements and organizations which bound together people with common ideals of evangelizing the world. In the era before ecumenism these movements and organizations were strictly for Catholics only. So the young Christian Workers founded by a Belgian priest, Cardign, aimed to evangelize the world of work, in particular the workplaces of young men and women. It was rooted in the Catholic faith of Europe; it set out to address the situations in the factories and workshops of the Europe of the time.

They were places which often destroyed and degraded the young men and women who produced the polished products which made the owners rich. It was a powerful movement which dynamically transformed the young men and women, as much as it transformed factories and workshops. It led also to the growth of the priest worker movement. It has declined in the modem Church because the factories and workshops have been closed in many areas (and opened in Asia). In their place are service industries and high technology. In the factories that remain, robots do the jobs which were previously done by the young workers. Too often the young workers join the dole queue.

In Britain the Catholic Evidence Guild used the outdoor platform to explain the teachings of the Church. Post war, the rise of ecumenism and the decline of interest in religion eliminated the Guild.

The Legion of Mary was a dynamic group of men and women united in the desire to bring Christ to the world, distinctive in that they saw themselves as figures of Mary the Mother of Jesus, living by the power of the Holy Spirit, and bringing her Son to the souls in need. Founded in 1921 by an Irishman working in the British Civil Service in Dublin, it spread rapidly. Legionaries went to Africa, Asia, South America, the Philippines and Soviet Russia. It was very highly and efficiently organized, and the organization was based on the handbook written and edited by Frank Duff the founder of the Legion. It is still a power in the Catholic Church, but does not attract the vibrant young people whom it inspired at one time to dedicate their lives to God and Mary through the Legion.

These three movements, the Catholic Evidence Guild, the Legion of Mary and the young Christian Workers, have all played a part in my own religious formation, especially the Legion of Mary. But, as with the religious Congregations, they had their beginnings, their springtime, their high summer and then autumn and the winter, when a small ageing group of former devotees keeps them going.

They all say their principles are eternal, but are they really the creation of a particular culture in a particular age?

In their place, and responding to a fast-changing world, new movements emerge. As with the previous creations they are the work of the Spirit of God moving in the Church of today, as the same Spirit moved in the Church of yesterday.

Among them are the Cursillo Movement founded by Edward Bonnin in Majorca in 1947, and now a world movement. It gathers men and women in a friendship group. At a key point in time they go to a retreat house or conference centre for a three-day course on Christianity, delivered mostly by a team of lay people. Those who have been through this three-day experience keep in contact with each other, and share their Christian life experiences. This movement has had a deep effect on me. It opened up for me, in a unique way, the depths of lay spirituality and showed me the power of an Internet of prayer.

But probably the most universal and energizing movement in the post-Vatican II Church is the Charismatic Movement. It reflects the state of the early Christian communities as described by St Paul in 1 Cor.12 – the gifts of the Holy Spirit poured out in abundance. It results in lives being transformed, in vibrant liturgies full of joy. They sing and dance the praises of God, often to the music of guitars, keyboards and drums. It develops prayer groups. It is fully ecumenical, sharing its riches with brothers and sisters in other religions. I have never been involved with the Charismatic Movement as such; I have never been 'baptised in the Spirit' (a phase I dislike); I have never had 'the gift of tongues' and have not felt any desire to be gifted like that. But people have told me, and I believe them, that baptism in the Spirit is a very profound spiritual experience, and on the occasion when I have heard a large group singing in tongues, I have found it very beautiful and very moving.

So, I was not perturbed at the thought of meeting the New Dawn group; but I was anxious in case Walsingham was so packed with New Dawn people that there would be no room for little me.

Meanwhile I was trying to cope with the A148, the road to Fakenham. There was no pavement. I was a helpless, frightened little rucksack man facing the oncoming traffic as it passed me at a distance of twelve inches to twenty-four inches away. Swish, swish, swish it went past, endless, without a break, I got a fleeting glimpse of grim faces huddled over steering wheels and other faces trapped inside the pressed steel boxes dressed in pressurized paint which hurled towards me and vanished. And I was out in the open air where the sun was shining, and the grass was growing and the birds were singing, and for all my fear I would not have changed places. Despite that, along every border of this kind of road which I walked in this long journey, there lay corpses of rabbits and squirrels and birds. I saw thousands of dead animals, and I am not exaggerating; and I knew I could be another roadside statistic if I made a wrong move, or a driver did. I wanted out of this deadly road to Fakenham, and after two and a half miles I turned left on to a side road to West Newton on the edge of the Sandringham estate. Now I was moving in a different world and I was singing.

The Queen spends a lot of time at Sandringham, and it is easy to understand why. It is an oasis of tall shady trees, little ponds and lakes and many ancient pathways. There were few cars on the narrow road and some young girls on horseback passed me and waved. These lanes were made for this kind of traffic and for the young girls on horses. They rode them so easily, and were dressed in bright clothing, with helmets on their heads, with long hair streaming down their backs.

I took a farm track to Anmer and stopped on it to eat the sandwich which Josie had carefully wrapped for me some hours earlier. Henry and Josie had celebrated fifty years of marriage some weeks before I arrived and the house had been filled with cards from well-wishers. Josie had also filled a flask for me, and she poured the tea out of an exquisite silver teapot that belonged to a more affluent age. I noticed this, and also the period furniture which filled the house. It was exceedingly elegant, and I asked Josie about it. She told me that the house and its contents had been bequeathed to Henry by his father.

After leaving West Newton I did not meet a single person except two young cyclists with saddle packs. I had met them yesterday on the road to King's Lynn pushing against the wind. They had stopped and talked about it, and I guessed they were from Scandinavia. They passed me as I ate and drank tea. They told me that they were making for the Peddars Way, which is a long-distance footpath running straight as a Roman road through the whole length of Norfolk, south to north, and ending at the sea at Hunstanton. The name suggests that it was an ancient pilgrims' way to Walsingham. Later I took a photograph of it where it crossed my own ancient footpath. After that brief encounter I was alone with the trees, the hedges, the rabbits and the birds. with the wild flowers growing on the verges.

An electric storm developed suddenly, and the rain came down like a curtain. I put on all my protective clothing and pushed on gaily. In the rain the dry land came alive, smelling of wet grass and a delicious freshness, and as the rain died away and the sun came out, I emerged on to a tarmacadamed road right opposite the King's Head.

I waited in the garden for the proprietor to arrive. Inside the hotel a big Alsatian (this time a canine!) barked at me. He was only doing his job, and I saluted him, safe behind the locked door. A big car drew up and the proprietor and his wife emerged. He showed me the en suite bedroom where I would spend the night. It was luxurious and fairly expensive, but I did not mind now; my journey was almost over. The soup they served that night was delicious and the bread was real bread. I was overcome by happiness. It all seemed too good to be true. That night I had a dream; it was a dark dream, very threatening. Something evil and deadly was approaching me, and I woke up before it reached me. The sun was shining in my bedroom at 6 a.m. I dismissed the dream from my mind. This was the day I would reach Walsingham.

The proprietor of the King's Head was a big Italian. He looked like Pavarotti without the beard and smile. He must have lost his smile somewhere along the path of life and I do not think he was able to speak fluent English. If he did he was reluctant to communicate with me. But his cooking was excellent, and I guess it was a hotel which attracted gourmets, and one glance at me would tell him that I was not in that kind of league.

His daughter was a pleasant girl with an Anglo-Italian face. She served behind the bar. There was also a tall young man whom I guessed to be his son. The Alsatian was friendly in a doggy kind of way, but after his initial communication behind the locked door he contented himself with sniffing me all over and must have come to the same conclusion as his master, that I was not one of his eye-catching paw-stretching gourmets, and he lost interest in me.

Outside the hotel window the countryside was veiled in a mist brought on by the heavy rain which had fallen in the night. Weak morning sunlight was beginning to filter through, and the pools on the tarmac of the drive were successively dark ponds and radiant mirrors, with myriads of tiny flies moving busily to and fro like Saturday shoppers at Tesco. It was time for me to pack the rucksack carefully for the last time, with weatherproofs strapped in the top. I put on the boots, walked downstairs and paid the bill with a credit card, and went out for the final miles.

Chapter 23

Walsingham

It was a cold day. The rain had done too much and the long hot days were over. I took the B1165 out of Bircham. I was making for a footpath through a wood near a place called Barmer. The road was wet and after days of hot sunlight the oil spills on the road made it treacherous. I was aware of this and kept well away from the edge, walking on tufty grass at the side. It was not a busy road by our standards, but any A, B, or C road is now bounced over by vehicles in the England of 1996, and there's no peace on them.

Suddenly a big car passing me at speed braked. It screamed around on the road and for a split second I thought it would hit me. It then turned a full circle and crashed on the bank opposite me. I froze. A car coming from the opposite direction stopped just a few feet away from the stranded car. Its door opened and a man emerged looking very dazed. He seemed to be in his mid-sixties, florid face and uncertain on his feet. I went over and asked him if he was all right. I also apologized if I had been to blame, for apparently I was near the entrance to his driveway. He shook his head 'No,' he said. 'It was my fault. I had gone too far and put the brake on suddenly; then the car skidded.' He was still very shaken.

Out of the other car came a young woman, round-faced, dark-skinned, Burmese in appearance. She was concerned for the man. I gathered she was in the medical profession, and could be a doctor. But he assured her also that he would be all right.

The tyre had burst on the car, but he backed out of the bank, and limped the car into the driveway, with the ribboned tyre flat on the road and the exhaust scraping sparks off the tarmacadam like a man striking matches.

One mile later I turned off through the woods on a footpath. All through this pilgrimage I had been conscious of Guardian Angels. This day I thanked and praised my own special one who had taken care of me and guarded me. I had been aware of special helps at special moments, many of them in the form of people who had been kind and considerate to the little stranger in a way I had not met before. Many of them I have mentioned in this account. But in addition to them there was the constant awareness of being looked after in a way I find hard to define.

The term 'insurance' would be wrong. It was not written on paper; I did not sign anything. It was inside me and all around me, and I knew it. And from this moment onwards, until I reached the Slipper Chapel, I walked through deserted and beautiful lanes. No more dead rabbits and birds. No more stinking fuel fumes. No more swish, swish, swish of speeding cars and the hideous HGVs with diesel-fumes fighting to get in my lungs, thundering past and blowing my hat off.

Just silence. Birds and trees and the wet grass. Miles of silence and the beauty, as though I was on the outskirts of the Garden of Eden. Squirrels did somersaults on tree boughs, rabbits rabbitted in the undergrowth, frogs croaked in the wet grass, ants marched on indignantly. I felt like Snow White in the Walt Disney film and everything about me was singing. So I said the Joyful mysteries and loved every bead of them.

I had brought no food, because I guessed I would reach Walsingham soon after midday. I kept putting on my weatherproofs and taking them off when the rain stopped. Finally I left them on because it was cold enough to have extra plastic around what was left of me. And I passed below South Creake to North Barsham. Then the sun came out and I took off my plastic, beneath a signpost which read 'Slipper Chapel 1/8 mile'.

Then suddenly around the corner I saw the meadow on the left-hand side covered with cars. Beyond it a further meadow covered in marquees, for all the world like parsley sauce at the edge of a big dinner plate prepared for robots from the Halewood factory.

112

A car window rolled down and Fr Gerry Kelly shouted, 'Hello.' Then another car with Frank and Pat and Mary Mac in it. They got hold of me like a teddy bear. I just could not believe it: but neither could they. I had been hoping to come in here unnoticed and anonymous, because this pilgrimage was very personal and private. But this was not to be. There must have been three thousand people at this New Dawn Conference, and I had to run right into the middle of it, and too many knew me.

But I shook them off because I needed to pray on my own. And, rucksack on my back, I went into the Slipper Chapel. It was so luminous: an ancient building going back to the mists of time. And there at the side was the Mother of God surrounded by flowers and candles.

And I said something to her.

And she said something to me.

But what I said to her, and what she said to me is our secret.

I only knew that I was crying without shame.

St Mary's Woolton, 1963. Way out, after Mass.

Left: Fr Harris (later Bishop Harris), centre: Fr Jimmy, right: Fr Malone

Stella and John   page 83

Housekeeper   page 95

I decided I would not risk it; dark and evil thoughts were running through my head and I had to talk to myself. 'Listen, YOU, this is a pilgrimage, not a crusade to open footpaths.'   page 86

In the beautiful medieval church at Holbeach, built two hundred years before the Reformation, is a tomb surmounted by a stone figure of a knight in full armour and by his side the stone carving of a severed head.
page 99

First sight of King's Lynn, but much to walk and a bridge to cross. I knew now that nothing, barring an accident, could stop me from reaching Walsingham. page 101

Just silence. Birds and trees and the wet grass. Miles of silence and the beauty as though I was on the edge of the Garden of Eden. page 112

Waughs Well.   page 140

The road dwindles to a narrow footpath on a contour. High Hill along
Grain Brook and cross footbridge. Waughs Well on the right, and a
reservoir below on the left.   page 140

Fr Jimmy – a pilgrim on the Pennine Way.   page 149

Edale Cross, on the Pennine Way.   page 154

Wessenden Reservoir.

page 149

Leaving Monksdale. Then the track bends right and joins a minor road, which leads on to the B6049: turn right, and go down the road to Millers Dale.

page 157

At this point you leave the Limestone Way. You emerge into the square
of the village, opposite an ancient stone cross, with the Kings Head Inn
in the background. page 165

Walk a short distance along the A6. The first road on the right is called Intake Lane. Turn into this and follow it as it rises steadily and becomes a footpath overlooking the Derwent, going through woodland. page 166

From the arch (or old rail bridge) in Intake Lane the Midshires Way follows the High Peak Trail across Derbyshire. At this point the lane becomes the Midshires Way going south. page 166

Wide grass verges were a help.

A Peak District scene.

From Morkery Wood, and up to the dismantled railway: the footpath goes through the wheatfields.   page 187

A pilgrim to Walsingham.

Turn left and walk some 300 yards to a Public Footpath and bridle path.

page 203

Go north when the bridle path reaches the Peddars Way.

page 205

Mary of Walsingham ...
Meet me in the Slipper Chapel,
Take me to your heart.

Part II

The Pilgrimage Route

A Pilgrimage

The idea of pilgrimage is part of the Christian heritage. The account of 'salvation history' bases itself on the history of the chosen people, the children of Abraham. It gives us the needed insight into our Creator, the God who loves, through the successive epochs of human history. It is knowledge not from reasoning or from dogmatic assertions, but recognizing the work of God in human life. The first pilgrimage is that of Abraham himself, called by God to leave his home and the place where his people lived and go to an unknown land. But the most spectacular is that of the freeing of the people of Israel from the slavery in Egypt. They cross the Red Sea and enter a desert, and they trek for forty years in the wilderness, making for a promised land. It is in this momentous journey that they are formed by God into a single people, and receive the laws and customs which have moulded them until this present day.

So there are certain fixed elements in pilgrimage.
1   A journey
2   Very often with company
3   To a promised place
4   Involving hardship, penance.
5   For a religious purpose, or in fulfilment of a vow.

Pilgrimage, then is deeply rooted in our Christian heritage, and this pilgrimage to Walsingham is of that nature. And in the three or four days taken to traverse the section of the Pennine Way every pilgrim will understand that this is a

117

penitential exercise, for he/she will be traversing long sections of difficult moorland terrain, some of it involving unpleasant peat troughs, and over the gritstone landscape of the high Pennines. Yet, when they have finished this section , and later look back on the experience, they will understand that their bodies and spirits have been purified by the experience. There is a special quality in the bleak moorlands and the lonely footpaths of this section which is unique, penitential and uplifting. In this section they experience a forgiveness of sin and a purification of soul, which prepares them for the gentle and beautiful to be found in Derbyshire, Lincolnshire and Norfolk. It is the prelude to the joy of entering Walsingham as a pilgrim.

Useful Information

Helpful Hints In Preparation

You need the correct clothing for such a long distance walk. Consult somewhere like Outdoor World.

Maps are important. The maps provided are a guide to the route. But if you lose your way, you may need a full scale map of the area. I will indicate the maps for each area. So each stage of the route needs careful preparation.

I suggest that you use the Ordnance Survey maps, Landranger. They cover the distances. You do not need many. Buy them new, because the older maps do not have the newly opened footpaths whereas the new ones do. I suggest particularly Landranger nos. 109, 110, 129, 130 and 131. I think it would be well to get a copy of the Midshires Way, and the Limestone Way. These are available in leaflet form from various outlets contained in Information Services. I suggest looking at someone's copy of Wainwright's *Pennine Way* Book; no need to buy a separate copy; someone will lend one. You do not need to carry it. Add in Landranger no. 132 covering the King's Lynn to Walsingham area, and you have enough to be certain of keeping on the route.

To determine overnight stay is a difficulty. Except for youth hostels it is better not to book ahead. You are putting a programme together in advance which you have to keep to in order to reach a B & B. The best way is to phone the morning you leave one base, to secure the next one for the evening. The various information centres in the major tourism towns you will be passing will tell you the names

119

and phone numbers of available B and Bs. Phone one, and book then.

I append a list of Information Centres you can use.

Carry in your rucksack also a copy of the Morning and Evening Prayer of the Church. Finish each day with the Evening Prayer of the Church. Carry a rosary so that during the morning you can recite the Joyful Mysteries, the Sorrowful in the afternoon, and the Glorious in the evening.

Lastly, carry a copy of one of the Gospels. They are available in paperback and are light to carry. Avoid any volume which is heavy or expensive. Inevitably they would be damaged by rain.

It may be difficult to find a Catholic Church for Sunday Mass. Consult your parish priest. For much of the journey you will be in villages remote from any Catholic Church. There are churches in Horwich and Ramsbottom. There is no Catholic church in Marsden. None in Edale, the nearest is Glossop. But there are Churches in Matlock, Belper, Melton Mowbray, Bourne, Spalding, Holbeach, Kings Lynn. Maybe the best you can do is to get leaflets of the Mass of the Sundays you will be on the road (two) and pray it in your bedroom as though you were there. But if access is impossible you have to accept it.

A mobile phone is a help. I did not use one; but I sometimes regretted it. Take a compass with your map and learn how to use the map and the compass. If you have no experience of mapreading with compass, please get a lesson in how to do it. It can save miles of frustrating walking if you can use one. In some cases it will keep you out of danger.

Every effort has been made to ensure the accuracy of the information on pp. 120–128.

Information Centres

Wigan. Trencherfield Mill, Wallgate, Wigan, WN3 4EL. Tel: 01942 825622

Rawtenstall. 41 /45 Kay Street, Rawtenstall, Lancashire BB4 7LS.
Tel: 01706 226590

Saddleworth. Saddleworth Museum, High Street, Oldham OL3 6HS.
Tel: 01457 870336

Rochdale. The Clock Tower, Town Hall, Rochdale, Lancashire OL16 1AB.
Tel: 01706 356592

Holmfirth. 49–51 Huddersfield Road, Holmfirth, West Yorkshire HD7 1JP.
Tel: 01484 222444

Glossop. The Gatehouse, Victoria Street, Glossop, Derbyshire SK13 8HT.
Tel: 01457 855920

Matlock. Crown Square, Matlock, Derbyshire DE3 3AT.
Tel: 01629 583388

Matlock Bath. The Pavillion, Matlock, Derbyshire DE4 3NR.
Tel: 01629 55082

Bakewell. Old Market Hall, Bridge Street, Bakewell, Derbyshire DE45 1DS.
Tel: 01629 813227

Derby. Assembly Rooms, Market Place, Derby, Derbyshire DE1 3AH.
Tel: 01332 255802

Loughborough. Town Hall, Market Place, Loughborough, Leicestershire LE11 3EB.
Tel: 01509 218113

Sleaford. The Mill, Money's Yard, Carre Street, Sleaford, Lincolnshire NG34 7TW.
Tel: 01529 414294

Melton Mowbray. Windsor House, Windsor Street, Melton Mowbray, Leicestershire LE13 1BU.
Tel: 01664 480992

Stamford. The Arts Centre, 27 St Mary's Street, Stamford, Lincolnshire PE9 2DL.
Tel: 01780 755611

Spalding. Ayscoughfee Hall Museum, Churchgate, Spalding, Lincolnshire PE11 2RA.
Tel: 01775 725468

King's Lynn. The Custom House, Purfleet Quay, King's Lynn, Norfolk PE30 1HP.
Tel: 01553 763044

Fakenham. Red Lion House, Market Place, Norfolk NR21 9BY.
Tel: 01328 851981

Norwich. The Guildhall, Gaol Hill, Norwich, Norfolk NR2 1NF.
Tel: 01603 666071

Suggested Accommodation en route

Lancashire
Red Lion. Parbold, Wigan, Lancashire. Tel: 01257 462336

Parr Hall Farm. Parr Lane, Eccleston, Chorley, Lancs.
Tel: 01257 451917

The Poplars. 58 Horseshoe Lane, Bromley Cross, Nr Egerton.
Tel: 01204 308001

Globe Farm Guest House. Huddersfield Road (A62), Delph, Nr Oldham.
Tel: 01547 873040

Derbyshire (Pennine Way)
White House. Holthead, Slaithwaite, Huddersfield HD7 5TY.
Tel: 01484 842245

Boothstead Farm. Rochdale Road, Denshaw, Oldham, OL3 5UE.
Tel: 01457 878622

*Guest House.*Waters Road, Marsden, Huddersfield HD7 6NG.
Tel: 01484 844235

Forest Farm. Mount Road, Marsden, Huddersfield HD7 6NN.
Tel: 01484 842687

Middle Hills Farm. Grange Mill, Matlock, Derbyshire DE4 4HY.
Tel: 01629 650368

Barleycorn Croft. Sheldon, Bakewell, Derbyshire DE45 1QS.
Tel: 01629 813636

Home Farm. Ible, Grange Mill, Matlock, Derbyshire DE4 4HS.
Tel: 01629 650349

Mandale House. Haddon Grove, Bakewell, Derbyshire DE45 1JF.
Tel: 01629 812416

Graystones. Sunny Bank Lane, Tideswell, Buxton, Derbyshire SK17 8JY.
Tel: 01298 871591

The Old Toll House. Cressbrook, Buxton, Derbyshire
SK17 8SY.
Tel: 01298 872547

Housley Cottage. Foolow, Hope Valley, Derbyshire S32 5QB.
Tel: 01433 631505

Chy-an-Dour. Vicarage Lane, Ashford in the Water,
Bakewell, Derbyshire DE45 1QN.
Tel: 01629 813162

Brookfield Guest House. Brookfield Barber Booth,
Edale S33 7ZL.
Tel: 01433 670227

Midlands
*Alambie.*189 Main Road, Morley, Derby DE7 6DG.
Tel: 01332 780349

Laurel Farm. Stanton-on-the-Wolds, Keyworth, Notts
NG12 5BL.
Tel: 0115 937 3488

White Lodge Farm. Kettleby, Melton Mowbray,
Leicestershire LE14 3JB.
Tel: 01664 822286

Gorse House. Grimston, Melton Mowbray, Leicestershire
LE14 3BZ.
Tel: 01664 813537

Bryn Barn. Waltham-on-the-Wolds, Melton Mowbray,
Leicestershire LE14 4AH.
Tel: 01664 464783

Lincolnshire / Norfolk
*The Pingles.*Thurlby, Bourne, Lincolnshire PE10 0EX.
Tel: 01778 394517

Westgate House. Whaplode, Spalding, Lincolnshire PE12 6RU.
Tel: 01406 370546

Cackle Hill House. Holbeach, Spalding, Lincolnshire PE12 8BS.
Tel: 01406 426721

Bakers Cottage. Docking, King's Lynn, Norfolk, PE31 8LR.
Tel: 0485 518710

White Horse Inn. East Barsham, Fakenham, Norfolk NR21 0LH.
Tel: 01328 820645

Walsingham
Sue Ryder Care Centre. Old Vicarage, Little Walsingham, Walsingham, Norfolk NR 22 6DF.
Tel: 01328 824400

Elmham House. Little Walsingham, NR22 6EG.
Tel: 01328 820217

St David's House. Friday Market, Little Walsingham, Norfolk, Walsingham, Norfolk NR22 6BY.
Tel: 01328 820633

Hostels and Youth Centres

Stones Centre. Ripponden, Sowerby Bridge, West Yorkshire HX6 4LA.
Tel: 01422 823514

Forest Farm Bunk House. Marsden, Huddersfield HD7 6NN.
Tel: 01484 842687

Crowden Youth Hostel. Crowden, Glossop, Derbyshire SK13 1HZ.
Tel: 01457 852135

Edale YHA. Rowland Cote, Nether Booth, Edale S33 7ZH.
Tel: 01433 670302

Hallowford Centre. Castleton, Hope Valley, S33 8WB.
Tel: 01433 620377

Castleton YHA. Castleton Hall, Castleton, Hope Valley
S33 8WG.
Tel: 01433 620235.

Ravenstor YHA. Miller's Dale, Buxton, Derbyshire
SK17 8SS.
Tel: 01298 871826

Bakewell YHA Hostel. Fly Hill, Bakewell, Derbyshire
DE45 1DN.
Tel: 01629 812313

Youlgreave YHA. Fountain Square, Youlgreave, Derbyshire
DE45 1UR.
Tel: 01629 636518

Elton YHA. Elton Old Hall, Main Street, Elton, Derbyshire
DE4 2BW.
Tel: 01629 650394

Matlock YHA and Training Centre. Matlock, Derbyshire
DE4 3NF.
Tel: 01629 582983

Shining Cliff Youth Hostel. Ambergate, Belper, Derbyshire
DE56 2RE.
Tel: 07788 725938

St John's College. Bramcote, Beeston, Nottingham NG9 3DS.
Tel: 0115 925 1114

Brooksby College. Brooksby, Melton Mowbray,
Leicestershire LE14 2LJ.
Tel: 01664 434291

Thurlby. YHA. 16 High Street, Thurlby, Lincs PE10 0EE.
Tel: 01778 425588

King's Lynn YHA. King's Lynn, Norfolk, PE30 1JB.
Tel: 01553 772461

Catholic Churches

Coppull. St Oswalds. Mass – Sat. 6.30pm Sun. 8.30 am.
10.30am.
Tel: 01257 79208

Horwich. St Mary's. Mass – Sun. 8.30. 11.00 am. 6.30pm.
Tel: 01204 468209

Ramsbottom. St Joseph's. Mass – Sat. 6.00 pm Sun. 9.30.
Tel: 01706 823200

Glossop. St Mary's. Mass – Sun. 10.00 am.
Tel: 01457 853124

Rochdale. Sacred Heart. Mass – Sat. 6.30 pm. Sun. 9.00
am. Tel: 01706 45603
St John the Baptist. Mass – Sat. 5.30pm. Sun. 10.00am
Tel: 01706 646877

Tideswell. Immaculate Heart of Mary. Mass – Sun. 9.30am.
Served from Chapel-En-Le Frith. Tel: 01298 813491

Bakewell. English Martyrs. Mass – Sun. 9.30 am.
Tel: 01629 640241

Matlock. Our Lady and St Joseph. Mass – Sat. 6.00 pm.
Sun 8.00 am. Tel: 01629 582804

Belper. Our Lady of Perpetual Succour. Mass – Sat. 6.30
pm. Sun. 10.00 am. Tel: 01773 822182

Duffield. St Margaret Clitheroe. Mass – Sun. 8.30 am.
Tel: As Belper.

Borrowash. St Hugh's. Mass – Sun. 9.15 am. 11.00 am.
Tel: 01332 673562

Melton Mowbray. St John the Baptist. Mass – Sat. 6.00 pm.
Sun. 9.00 am. Tel: 01664 562274

Stamford. St Mary and St Augustine. Mass – Sat. 6.00 pm.
Sun. 9.00 am. 11.00 am. Tel: 01780 762010

Bourne. St Gilbert. Mass – Sat. 6.00 pm Sun. 8.45 am.
Tel: 01778 423593

Spalding. Immaculate Conception and St Norbert.
Mass – Sat. 4.45 Sun. 10.30 am. Tel: 01775 722056

Holbeach. Holy Trinity. Mass – Sat. 6.30 pm. Sun. 9.30 am.
Tel: 01406 423034

King's Lynn. Our Lady of the Annunciation. Mass – Sat.
6.00 pm. Sun. 8.00 am. 11.00 am. Tel: 01553 772220

Horrock Hall to Adlington

Map 1

1. At High Moor Lane turn right and continue walking to the entrance of Horrock Hall estate. Follow this road (O.K. for walkers not drivers) until the road bends to the right towards Horrock Hall.

2. Here at the bend in the road the large sign leads you to the footpath mast clearly seen above you. From this point also you can see the top of Winter Hill with the tall telecommunication masts. This is where we are going. It is directly east, meanwhile walk on past the mast.

3. At Mill House farm, turn right at a narrow road and follow for half a mile, turn left – again for half a mile – until you meet the junction with Tunley Lane, continue down Tunley Lane up to a footpath sign on your left. This leads you to the road to Mossy Lea. Turn left on this road for 200 yards. Turn right at the first of two footpath signs,

4. The path goes through to the United Reformed Church and continues as a narrow lane – Chisnall Lane. It crosses the motorway by a footbridge.

5. After the footbridge there are three routes: left, right or centre. The right begins immediately descending steps and a handrail steeply down to a path in woodland. Take the centre route; it is a well-defined path; both routes lead to Preston Road (A49). This path leads past the relic of the Chisnall Coal Pit. Turn right and go down the road until you meet the first footpath sign on the left. Take it and it bends in a U-turn left, right, and right again to Bogburn Hall Farm. There go left through the farm buildings to the Chorley Road (A5106) a mile on. Cross the road: slightly left is the road to Adlington.

6. Come out on the Chorley–Wigan road. Just on the right down the road is the pub called the White Crow. Almost opposite is the sign (hidden by bushes) To Adlington – Footpath. Take this. Follow the power lines. The stiles are not modern but are adequate. Brook on the right hand side.

7. Follow the track. It comes to some houses and becomes more of a solid track. It reaches a tarmac road; turn right here for a short distance and then left at Old School Lane. Short tarmac road. Last house on the left is an old school house built in 1515. Take footpath again just past it, over a stile into a lane; two stiles and then a valley with a stream at the bottom in woodland.

Horrock Hall to Adlington

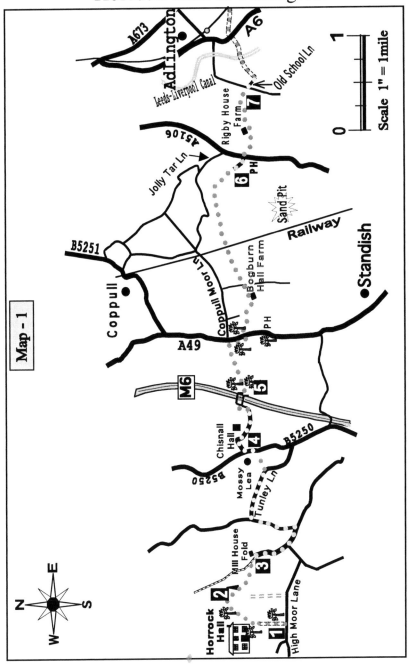

Map - 1

Scale 1" = 1mile

Adlington to Belmont

Map 2

1. Follow the track. It comes to some houses and becomes more of a solid track. It reaches a tarmac road; turn right here for a short distance and then left at Old School Lane. Short tarmac road. Last house on the left is an old school house built in 1515.

2. Take footpath again just past it: over a stile into a lane; two stiles and then a valley with a stream at the bottom in woodland, take stile in left-hand corner down by the river, follow the path by the river, over stiles. Come to a sign pointing straight ahead. Ignore the one going left and up and follow the river under the bridge of the canal in an easterly direction. At an intersection where a footbridge leads over the river, ignore the footbridge and continue in an easterly direction through two wooden posts. See a tall chimney and go towards it; some terraced houses on the rise on the left. Then, as the river vanishes under factory buildings, climb up to the road at the Wagon and Horses. Left for approximately 100 yards to the Railway Inn. Footpath sign on the right.

3. Huyton Road. It winds around the factory complex and you see a small road on the right, which is probably the original Huyton Road.

4. It leads past a pond on the right just past the factory buildings and passes under the railway. Follow sign posts – 'Adlington Walks' to a footpath alongside the river going sharp right (over a fallen tree!) It leaves the river and turns up

132

left (Adlington Walks sign indicate), following a brook up the fell side. At one point the sign indicates crossing the brook on the left. Keep sharp lookout for it; it is about 150 yards up the fell. After some yards you cross the brook again and rejoin the original path. Obviously some farmer had objected, hence the re-route. Path continues uphill to a tarmacadam road. Right opposite is a road called Shaws Drive. It leads to a path that continues straight up in an easterly direction.

5. It crosses the motorway by footbridge and winds through woodland by the side of a farm and comes out at a metal road opposite Rivington Conservation Centre. Turn Left down this road to the first road on the right – Horrobin Lane. This crosses the Higher and Lower Rivington Reservoirs and leads to a school, on the left of which is an open space which is used as a car park . This is the starting point for the next section – Rivington Pike and Winter Hill and beyond.

6. From car park by the Junior school, there is an opening on the right some 100 yards from the end of Horrobin Lane.

7. Go through car park to a bridleway. At tarmac road turn right and take road to Rivington Hall Barn (signposted). Follow path to the east of Barn to a footpath by a gate named Rivington. Trail goes up artificial steps of the Leverhulme buildings. To the tower below Rivington Pyke.

8. Turn left at the broad bridleway (Belmont Road) and continue for two miles to the main road.

9. Turn right 200 yards on, take the footpath on the left, via a stile and follow it all the way to Belmont. *Accommodation available at the Bull.* If going on, turn left up the road to the end of the reservoir and take the reservoir road on the right of the reservoir to a footpath leading to the Wilton Weavers Way.

Staying at Camping Barn of Rivington
For those who have had enough for one day! There is a camping barn on the edge of Rivington; it is the property of

the Water Board. Equire for use from the Water Board beforehand. To reach it, follow a footpath along the side of the Reservoir at the end of Horrobin Lane; it is the left side of Horrobin Lane. It leads to the Yarrow Reservoir. At the spot where the path forks, take the left fork and then a stile. Soon after crossing it take the path to the right. It skirts a deep ravine, wooded – and comes out on a farm road past Wilcocks farm. The barn is on the bend of the road on the right-hand side. It is just a barn; there are no farm buildings near it. Leaving the barn in the morning turn back down the farm road and take footpaths on left, leading to Sheep House Lane. Turn left when reached. After one and a half miles look for a stile on the left leading to Belmont. It is some two hundred yards past an unofficial car park on the left.

Adlington to Belmont

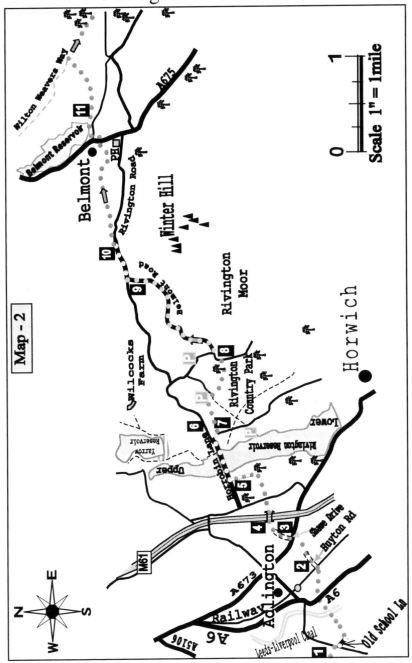

Dimple to Ramsbottom

Map 3

1. Go to the southern end of the reservoir and take the lane alongside it. It leads to a farm. (Three big dogs in separate kennels – all chained up hopefully.) Cross the stile through the farm buildings – waymarked. It leads to the broad footpath, the Wilton Weavers Way. Turn right and follow it downhill passing a wood on the left approximately a mile on. Here you reach a tarmac road.

2. Turn left down the road for about one hundred yards to a stile in the wall on the right hand side. – Follow the footpath downhill and go through the woodland. Large reservoir visible through the trees on the right. Come out by the Prince William Inn in Dimple. Cross the road to the road opposite. Proceed up this to the second stile on the left. This is the path to Chapeltown.

3. The Railway Road terminates at a busy highway. Turn left. Immediately you see that the highway divides. Take the right fork leading to Turton Bottoms. Follow this road through Turton Bottoms, past a signpost, past a pub. Birches Road,

4. Turn right along this cobbled road; come to a stone gateway and a tarmac road and some three or four detached houses recently built. On the right of the last house you see a footpath going up a flight of stone steps; take the path. It climbs steeply for a short time at the top there is a footpath waymarked on the left. Do not take it – go straight eastwards.

5. There is a tall chimney, (Peel Tower); it will be on your left-hand side as you follow the path. It leads to a group of houses on a tarmacadam road; come out at the side of a stone house.

6. Cross the road: opposite is a gateway and a farm track; there is no signpost, only a notice about cars not turning. Go through the gateway (no gate just gateposts) and follow the track uphill curving slightly to the right but always in an easterly direction. You will see a stile on the skyline, it looks like a white notice on the wall. It is an open stile with a white gate on hinges to keep the sheep in. Go through the stile, negotiate three other stiles going in the same direction; making four stiles in all.

7. Path ends at a farm on a hill: contour right, keeping the houses on the left. Go through a gate and join a path coming from a wood. Turn sharp left down by the side of a house to a green gate on the right and follow the path downhill. You will be looking at a valley, there is a footbridge in the distance over a stream. Make for it. Probably horses in the field by the footbridge. Cross the bridge and go uphill past a farm, keep the farm on your right, following the wall or wire fence until you come to a narrow tarmac road. Turn left on the road. After about one hundred yards see a signpost to the right. This leads to Range House.

8. The army territory, follow the path going east, unless the army flags are flying. If this is so take the path to the right. If the area is clear ignore the right footpath sign and continue going east; past a farm; the path swings to the left and down hill to cross the river.

9. It can be deep and there is no bridge. You are now on the outskirts of Ramsbottom. There is an indistinct path to the east going steeply uphill to a stile and a telegraph post. Or you can take the path along the river and turn left uphill for about five hundred yards downstream. Turn right down the road which these paths lead to.

10. It reaches a road, Lumb Carr Road. (B6214) – Turn left into Lumb Carr Road, then right into Chapel Lane, which runs into Tanners Street, then right into Carr Street.

Dimple to Ramsbottom

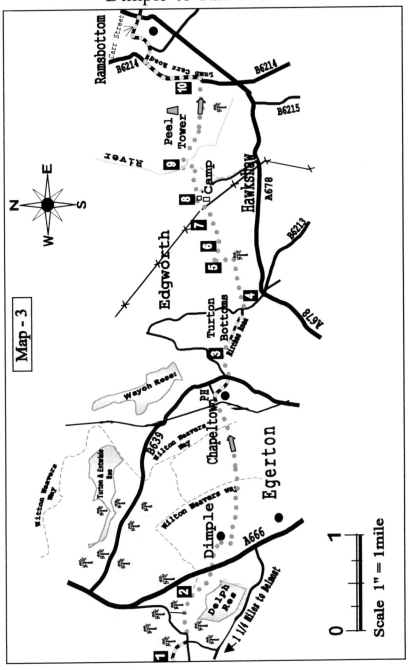

Map - 3

Scale 1" = 1mile

139

Ramsbottom to Whitworth

Map 4

1. Go downhill through the centre of Ramsbottom, past the Information Centre and a big pub. Cross the main road into Bridge Street and cross the river to Peel Brow and the weir. Follow the River Irwell north.

2. Go through a gate. Look at the wall on your right-hand side for a sign RW, which means Rossendale Way. Follow this it will branch right and cross the motorway (M66). Turn left and it will wind round to the Duckworth Arms on a main road. Turn right and after some two hundred yards you will see a signpost on the left (up the hill past a row of houses). It will be signposted Rossendale Way.

3. The crossing of the M66 after leaving Ramsbottom is by the Rossendale Way path. It comes in a short distance to the A56. Cross the A56 and pick up the signpost. Pickup two stiles and emerge at Bury Old Road, left for about one hundred yards, turn right down a narrow road with yellow markings on both sides.

4. At the A680 walk uphill for about a quarter of a mile. Signposted on left, Rossendale Way.

5. Follow, and come to ancient coal road. Goes east then turns north.

6. The road dwindles to a narrow footpath on a contour. Higher Hill along Grain Brook and cross footbridge. Waugh's

140

Well on the right and a reservoir below on the left. Continue to an intersection of paths: one going north with RW sign, one going west of it and one going east. Take the east path.

7. Pass through the extensive remains of a quarry and see the Cowpe Reservoir on the left and the whole extent of the Rossendale Valley. Pass Gragg High Level tank. Path turns south and after passing through a walled enclosure turn left for approximately two hundred yards. Then turn right at a disused quarry.

8. Cross the ford at Prickshaw brook. You are now above the Spring Mill reservoir which is on the right. The path skirts a housing estate. Look for the way on a path by the River Spoden.

9. Cross the A671 at its meeting with the B637. You are now in Whitworth.

Ramsbottom to Whitworth

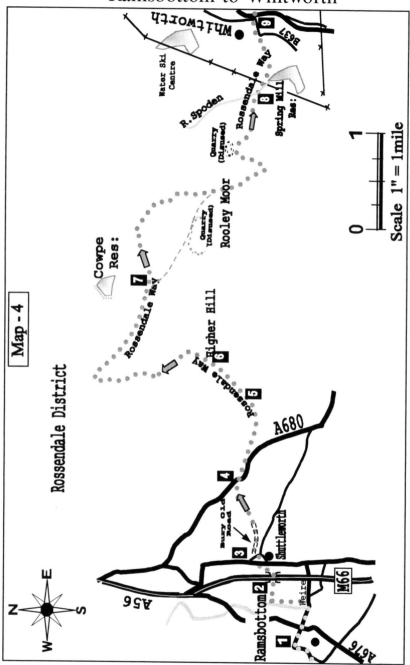

Map - 4

Rossendale District

Scale 1" = 1mile

Whitworth to the Whitehouse Pub

Map 5

1. Cross uphill; disused reservoir on the right and a golf course on the left. By the Golf Club, turn right by a pathway. Two paths intersect. Take the second path and go east to Barnfield Lane and path along the Watergrove Reservoir to the parking spot just below the reservoir wall.

2. From the car park. Leave the car park and walk around the reservoir in a northerly direction on the reservoir road, until reaching a signpost – Hollingworth – this goes to the right at 60 degrees uphill, good road, it passes through a gate on to the Hollingworth road going south; turn right along it for some yards. Midway between the gate you have just passed through and a stile in the wall, on the left is a faint path going uphill to the east, and making to a gap between two knolls.

3. It becomes an old lane and climbs steadily; you will see a ruined wall on the right, go through the two stone pillars of an ancient gateway and then turn left along the remnant of the wall. The path leaves the wall and goes upwards towards another ruined wall which you walk along. The path leaves the wall and climbs steadily in a south-easterly direction.

4. You will see the power lines on the right of you as you walk, striding across the hills and valleys. The path crosses an intersecting one and continues to the east, passes around a walled enclosure on the outside on to the open fell. You can see the radio and TV station in the distance which stands over the M62 motorway at its highest point.

5. Cross a small stream and the path follows the contour of the hill down towards a clear pathway on a fell, on the right hand it crosses a stream at the Turn Slack Clough and joins the broad pathway which seems to have some relationship to reservoir works and which contours around the hillside in an easterly direction, until you come to the wall of a farm. Keep on the outside of the path; see spire of the church and two small reservoirs. Come past an iron gate beside a scrap yard and come out at a house on another road (or street) called Lighthouse.

6. See bridleway opposite which goes at an angle from the road. It descends to a lower road. Turn left along this, past a row of houses and Stanfield Nursing Home. The road joins the main road through Summit and continues in the same direction. It is a fairly long stretch of road and gives one a chance to have a hot or cold drink. Almost at the end of the village on the far side of the road you will see a wooden green sign with nothing written on it pointing east besides a public house called the Summit.

7. Take that path; it goes over the Leeds and Liverpool canal into an open space used as a car park with large boulders blocking one of the entrances; there is a path on the left of this open space, it crosses a small stone bridge over a weir. There is a notice 'Summit Circuit Trail'. The path climbs left to higher ground and goes past the two Chelburn reservoirs.

8. After approximately a mile it crosses a reservoir drain and then a brook or stream at Castle Clough. At this point the path turns sharp right. Just at this bend take a path on the left (half hidden by foliage) It climbs steeply alongside the stream and past a small farm to join a bridleway which leads to a pub called the Whitehouse.

9. Opposite on the far side of the road is a signpost for the Pennine Way.

Ramsbottom to Whitworth

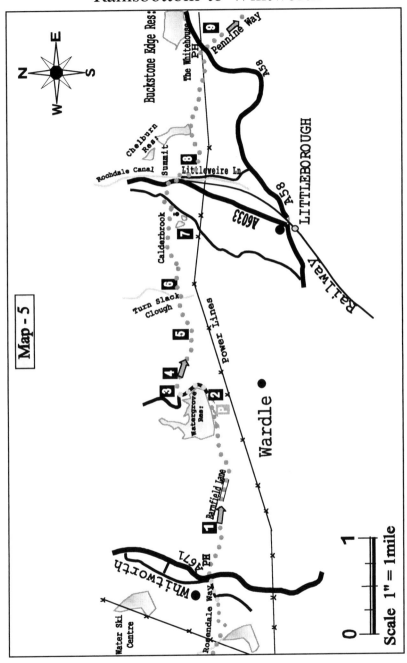

The Pennine Way
Whitehouse Pub to
Marsden/Standedge

Map 6

The Pennine Way. There are a great many books about this long-distance footpath. It is probably the best-known of all English pathways. It was the first long-distance one, and the forerunner of many others. One of your group will need to have read one of the books on it. It is 270 miles long: we walk the first 34 miles. Make sure you have a compass and a map or maps (Landranger 110, Ordnance Survey. Or OS Outdoor Leisure No. 1).

1. Cross the A58 road from the Whitehouse inn and going downhill for some yards see the Pennine Way fingerpost. It goes steeply up to a water channel following the contour of the hillside. Follow it to the rough cobbles of the Roman road going uphill. At the Aiggin Stone, a guide post of great antiquity, bearing carvings of a cross and initials, there is a gateway leading up to Blackstone Edge and the trig point, the white triangular on its highest point. The walking is easy on the gritstone. Follow the path from here in a southerly direction: now mercifully paved at its worse sections.

2. Cross the M62 by a narrow bridge; the path climbs again on the far side, passes by a huge TV mast, and turns left towards the A672; and reach the lay-by. You may find a van here selling burgers and hot drinks. Use it. These little gifts are life-savers.

3. Cross the road, the A672; Pennine Way sign: and follow the path over White Hill, passing another triangular marker on the highest point.

4. At this point there are two ways into Marsden. The first is to follow the Pennine Way as far as Standedge and cross the A62 (see map 7). This footpath crosses the moor and is very pleasant, swinging left of the Pennine Way after about a quarter of a mile and taking a footpath which curves left (east) to the outskirts of Marsden (The Standedge Trail).

4. Route two is the path which also starts at the A640, to the left of the Pennine Way. Follow on an old packhorse route (marked by packhorse stones) to a point where a beautiful high curved packhorse stone bridge crosses over a stream. Go over this and left on to a road which goes towards Marsden at the level of the valley. Follow for maybe a mile until you reach a pub at Tunnel End.

5. There turn right and follow straight up to the A62 and turn left downhill to Marsden. At the outskirts look for a junction of roads (row of shops ahead), Mount Road on right. Can take Old Mount Road, but better is the road which goes uphill across the street. It goes straight up to the public bridleway along the reservoirs. So does Old Mount Road, but it means going down steep steps to the valley floor and up again on the other side to reach the bridleway.

147

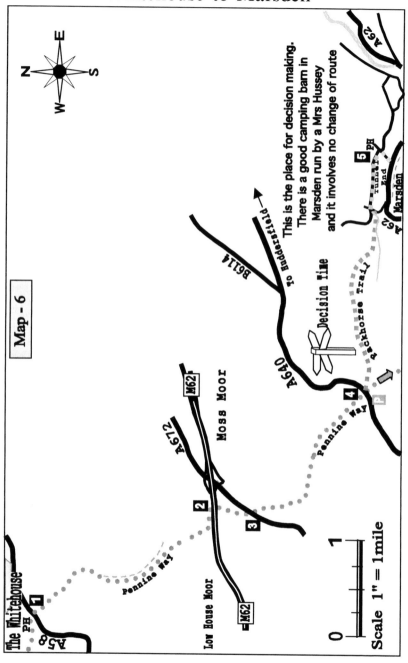

Map - 6

To Huddersfield →

This is the place for decision making.
There is a good camping barn in
Marsden run by a Mrs Hussey
and it involves no change of route

Decision Time

Packhorse Trail

Marsden

Tunnel End

PH 5

A62

B6114

A640

Pennine Way

M62

A672

Moss Moor

Low House Moor

M62

4

3

2

The Whitehouse

PH 1

A58

Pennine Way

N

Scale 1" = 1mile

0   1

148

The Pennine Way
Marsden/Standedge to Crowden

Map 7

1. The Pennine Way comes down from Standedge to the deep cutting where the road goes through to Huddersfield via Marsden. The way crosses the road to a rough road car park. On the left is the PW sign.

2. Another chance to go to Mrs Hussey's barn at Marsden. You may wish to spend the night here. After this there is no accommodation for some miles and the country is inhospitable, to put it mildly. At a junction of paths take the left-hand one. It is not too distinct so look for it (The Standedge Trail). It will cross a slight stream at a footbridge and turn towards Marsden. It reaches a secondary road. Turn right on this and keep to it. You will pass a B & B (on your left). Deep down in the valley on your right will be a primitive golf course.

3. There are four reservoirs, a string of them: Blakeley, Wessenden, Wessenden Head ... and the trail runs on the left of them, all the way to a minor road named, inevitably, Wessenden Head Road. To reach the track you need to see the Footpath sign, Public Footpath (but it may also have on it Kirklees Way). Follow this, keeping the reservoirs on your right-hand side. When you reach the minor road, about two miles on, turn right; it leads you to the A635 going across the moors to Huddersfield.

4. Cross the A635, and turn left for just a few yards to see a PW fingerpost pointing you to Black Hill. You may find a van selling hot drinks and other goodies. Don't pass it. You have a long way to go. Follow the PW uphill steeply. For part of the journey it is paved, thank God. (It wasn't in my day.) After some 45 minute of walking you come to an area of black peat and grit with no fixed signs. You need to take the compass and follow a bearing to the south-west. It is easy to get lost here. It is a wilderness and a dangerous wilderness. You need to find the triangular pillar standing in the middle of the wilderness, a white sign that someone did something constructive here. You leave it in a south-westerly direction. The PW will be found with some difficulty. It begins as a path marked only by the boot marks. Further down the hill you will see, thankfully, the paving stones again. Then you know you are on the right track. Difficult in mist.

Marsden to Black Hill (Crowden)

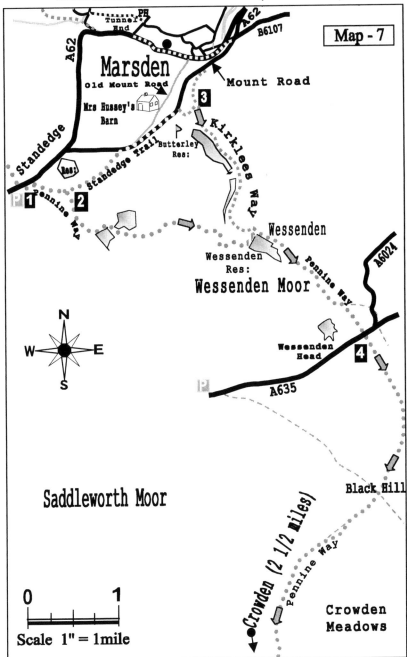

Map - 7

151

The Pennine Way
Crowden to the Snake Pass

Map 8

1. The paving stones runs along the hillside above Crowden brook. It climbs up to the Laddow rocks, becomes a narrow path: sometimes a nervous walker will move inland for safety. It descends gently into green fields.

2. If you are staying in the hostel at Crowden you turn left along the path beside the road. It is necessary to book lodgings at the hostel in good time. I suggest that you do this before the journey begins; some weeks before. The only accommodation is Glossop if the Crowden hostel is full.

3. If you are leaving for the final stage of this journey on the Pennine Way next morning, you leave the hostel and return on the path you used on the previous evening, This time it takes you south and crosses the road, and crosses the reservoir on a bridge, signposted. Then you begin the slow and tortuous climb to Bleaklow Head. (How apt these names are!)

4. Pass the Wain Stones and enter Hern Clough, into Devil's Dyke. Follow the stakes across the moor and come to the Snake Road (A57). Cross over into Featherbed Moss, and follow the stakes to Mill Hill and Ashop Head.

Crowden to the Snake Pass

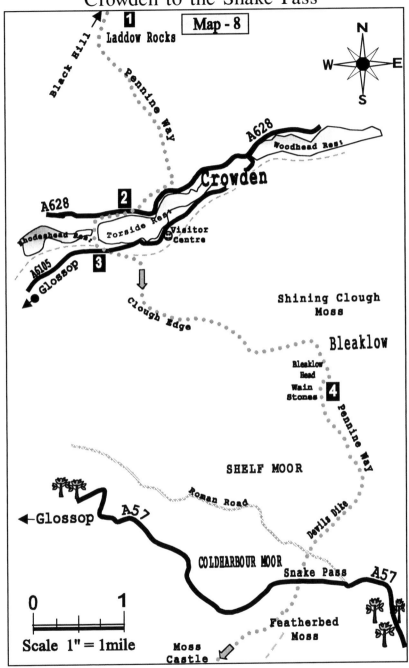

The Pennine Way
The Snake Pass to Edale

Map 9

1. At Devil's Dyke, follow the stakes across the moor and come to the Snake Road (A57). Cross over into Featherbed Moss, and follow the stakes to Mill Hill and Ashop Head.. Now you are entering the plateau of Kinder.

2. This all sounds easy, but in fact it is mile upon mile of slithering and stumbling where the paving stones have not yet been put in place and the peat groughs are implacable.

3. But the Kinder plateau is kinder, as its name implies and it leads past Kinder Downfall. Now you will see the shape of Kinder reservoir on the right, deep down in the valley, and the farmland around Hayfield. There is a convergence of paths, a crossroads. Going right for a short distance you reach the Edale Cross. This beautiful medieval relic is enclosed almost reverentially by the surrounding rocks.

4. But your path leads left, not right, so turn left from the Edale Cross and begin the long descent on the steps of Jacob's Ladder. On a fine evening you will see the first beauties of Derbyshire. Your penitential journey is almost over. The last decade of your rosary is the Glorious one; you are moving down to the softness of Edale. It has been a long day. It is probably better to stay the night at Edale and accommodation is usually available so long as you have followed the advice of phoning from Crowden before you set out.

Snake Pass to Edale

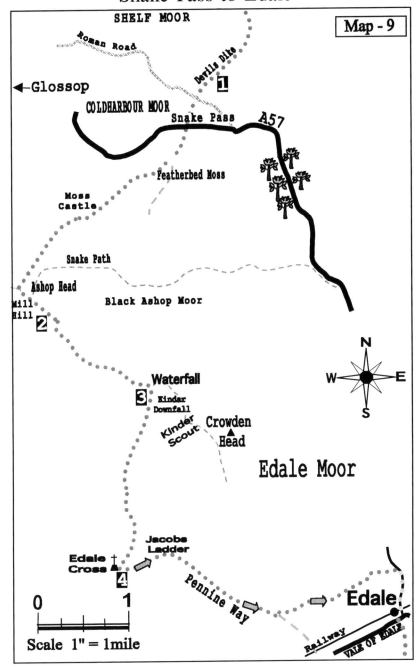

The Limestone Way
Edale to Millers Dale

Map 10

But if you are a macho walker, and it is still early afternoon you might want to pass through Edale and begin the three mile journey over the hill to Castleton. There are good accommodation and restaurants in Castleton. In that case, pass the National Park Information Centre ... well worth a visit if you need maps of the Limestone Way or accommodation advice: cross the road and take the signposted path to Hollins Cross and then drop down into Castleton.

1. Castleton is dominated by the ruins of the castle high up on the heights above it. It was built by Peveril, son of William the Conqueror in the eleventh century. You begin the LW by moving across the market place to the entrance of the Cave Dale.

2. There follows a 1500-metre climb up the escarpment to reach a wall on the right and a well defined track; reach a grass track, a bridleway signed 'Peak Forest'. Follow it across narrow road and intersecting footpaths and tiny enclosures, remains of ancient mines.

3. Reach the A623. Mount Pleasant Farm on your left. Turn left short distance up the A623, uphill.

4. At top of hill on the A623 turn right along the road to Wheston. About a mile on. following the LW marker, bear left into Haydale. Follow under line of oak trees. The Dale bends left to join the road.

5. Go right along the road for short distance. Turn left into Peter Dale, across a broad grass pasture. Difficult walking in the limestone. Take care in wet weather. Also allow time. It is a beautiful and memorable part of the walk. (You can go through Peter Dale and into Monksdale,) but leave it before Miller's Dale, because you cannot easily get out of Millers Dale.

6. It is imperative to leave the limestone clints by Monksdale House, Pass Monksdale Farm on the right. Then the track bends right and joins a minor road, which leads on to the B6049: turn right, and go down the road to Millers Dale.

7. There is a B & B in Millers Dale and a good inn near the viaduct, by the side of the river.

The Limestone Way
Edale to Millers Dale

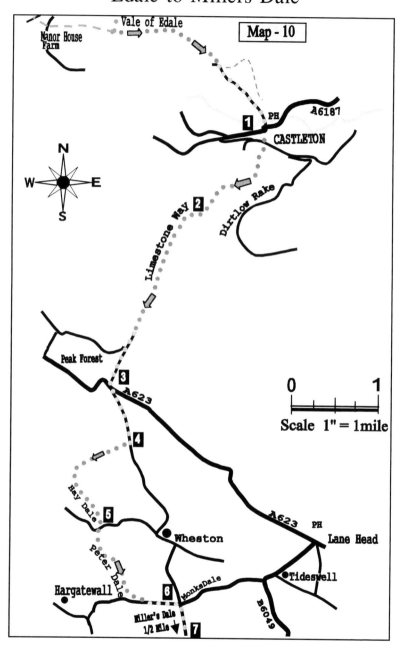

The Limestone Way
Millers Dale to Monyash

Map 11

1. There is a B & B in Millers Dale and a good inn near the viaduct, by the side of the river.

2. Go west down the B6049 passing St. Anne's Church on the right, and pass under the great viaduct. Soon after the road has crossed the bridge over the river Wye, turn left into Long Lane and follow it to a road. Turn right and reach cross roads. Continue into Priestcliffe Road, (leads to A6) opposite Waterloo Inn.

3. Cross the A6 and take Sough Lane on the left of Waterloo Inn. Follow the lane uphill to a road. It is a very minor road. Turn right and follow it for a mile approx and see on the left LW waymarker. This is Green Lane, a metalled path which leads you to a crossroad. Go straight across towards the village of Flagg.

4. Town End Farm comes into view, pass it on right; pass church on the left. Stile on right (metal gate) Take path across the field. Another stile, path goes to middle of the next field and so to road. Road bends; after a right turn cross cattle grid to Knotlow Farm. Follow wall to stile in corner. Footpath signs: follow them; several paths meet.

5. Cross the first: the Limestone Way track is the next one, and it slants left. Follow to the road, turn right into Monyash. Walk along Chapel Street to crossroads.

159

6. Monyash is a beautiful little village. There is a pub, a village green, and an ancient stone cross. We find this setting in several of these Derbyshire villages. Go along Rakes Road. it swings left.

7. The Way goes between two farms; continues for more than half a mile. It becomes a footpath, then two stiles. Cross stile into Fern Dale.

8. Walk on the left of a wall. Cross another stile. Follow the path through a metal gate and turn right. Go down the drive (drive of One Ash Grange Farm). For those who need a sleep there is a camping barn further down.

Limestone Way – Millers Dale to Monyash (Youlgreave)

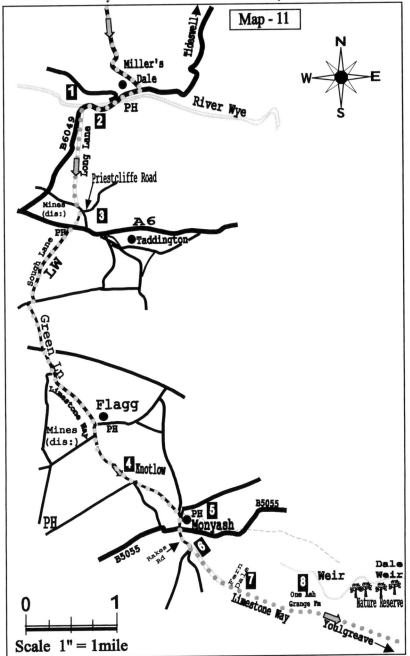

Map - 11

The Limestone Way
Monyash to Youlgreave on to the road for Bonsall

Map 12

1. Turn left after the Camping Barn. Cross a stile and turn right and go down limestone canyon into Cales Dale. Follow signpost to opposite side and climb steps. Follow the footpath signs to a road.

2. Follow the road towards a picnic site. Pass Moor Lane and take a stile on the right by a gate and follow the broad track by the side of picnic site. Go down left to the B5056. You may want to have a break, in which case go into Youlgreave village.

3. Turn left at the B5056. It goes round a bend and you will see a stile on the right which leads down to a lower road. Turn right along the road for half a mile. You will see Lomberdale Hall on your right and at an S-bend look for a track to the left which circles down to the river.

4. Cross the bridge over the river and follow the stream downstream by turning to the left. About 3/4 mile downstream cross river by a stone bridge. You now have the river on the right.

5. Another half mile: you reach a road and turn right to cross the bridge to the road. Walk up the road to a stile on your left. There will be four stiles on this footpath: it goes downhill and

162

up again; bear right and then left at rough stretch. You reach a gate with a stile by it. Turn immediately left and follow a track through woods to a road.

6. Turn right. Just short of the brow of the hill take a stile on the left, opposite a farm drive. You see two rocks set apart from each other known as Robin Hood's Stride. To the left of the path is a rocky prominence known as Crateliffe Rocks. There is an ancient cave once inhabited by a hermit. He carved a reproduction of the crucified Christ on the back wall of the cave. Go directly upwards between these two landmarks. At the top of the hill follow a footpath slightly left downhill to a gate.

7. Enter a lane directly ahead (Dudwood Lane). When it reaches the road (about half a mile) turn left, just a few yards, then turn right on a broad track. This track is about a mile long, it ends at a road, where you turn left and walk about forty yards.

Monyash to Youlgreave on to the road to Bonsall

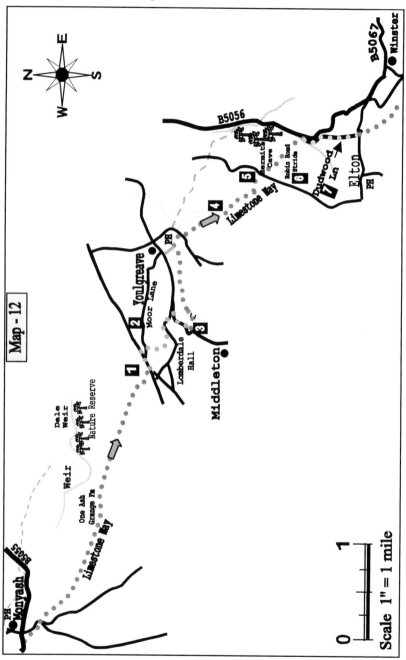

Scale 1" = 1 mile

The Limestone Way
the road for Bonsall, Cromford,
and the Midshires Way

Map 13

1. Cross at a junction of the road with the B5056 to a broad track which runs straight for half a mile.

2. When the track becomes a footpath and you see Luntor rocks, turn off the footpath and go down to the left to a stile on the right by a gateway, which you go through to the right. Follow over stiles to Bonsall Lane. Turn left down Bonsall Lane until you see a stile on the right and go diagonally across the field. You come to a point where two tracks cross.

3. At this point use your compass. Turn south along Blakelow Lane to a stile on the left. Turn half left to the first of six stiles leading to Moorlands Lane. Here a signpost sends you left to a further signpost about two hundred yards along, turn dead right and cross through six further stiles. Go around a ruin to a well-defined footpath and five more stiles! This makes you feel sympathy for the horses in the Grand National. But cheer up, you are near Bonsall. Follow the signpost to Upper Town and go down road into Bonsall.

4. At this point you leave the Limestone Way. You emerge into the square of the village, opposite an ancient stone cross, with the Kings Head Inn in the background. Turn left up Church Street, keeping the church on your right-hand side;

walk south. After some time the road becomes a footpath, waymarked. It rises on a grassy path.

5. Just over the top of the rise meet large iron gates ... two of them guarding the quarry in the background. Some distance on you see a similar gate, just one of them this time. Continue on the track for a short distance. You pass an opening in the woodland with paths going through the wood. Do not take this one; but move on a short distance on the track and see a larger opening in the woodland on your right, with the concrete remains of a roadway leading downwards. Opening on the left of this is a forest path (waymarked), which leads down to the A5012. Turn left and walk down to major road and into Cromford.

6. Greyhound Hotel on the corner. Cross the road (pedestrian crossing controlled by traffic light). Walk down to the A6 – Derby and turn right along it. (Coffee shops and bar meals possible in this area.)

7. Walk a short distance along the A6. The first road on the right is called Intake Lane. Turn into this and follow it as it rises steadily and becomes a footpath overlooking the Derwent, going through woodland.

8. Meet a signpost with the Midshires Way (two acorns on background of yellow circle on blue-grey). From the arch (or old rail bridge) in Intake Lane the Midshires Way follows the High Peak Trail across Derbyshire. At this point the lane becomes the Midshires Way going south. Continue along it, tuning right at a signpost waymarked and then sharp left in the direction of Belper. It turns sharp right and then left and continues on for nearly a mile, past a caravan park on your left, to cross into Longway Bank. Cross the B5035 road and up through a paddock to a path through woods.

The road to Bonsall, Cromford & the Midshires Way

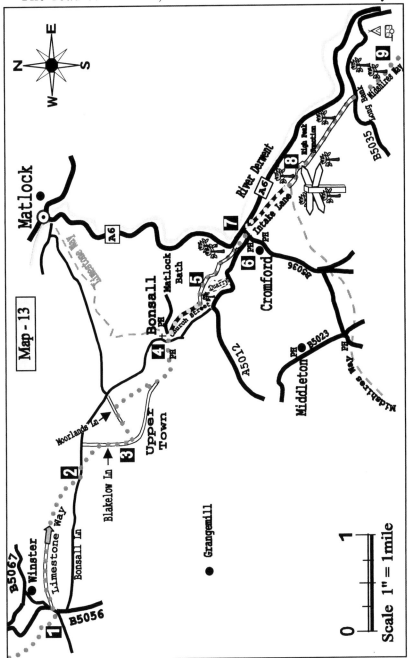

Map - 13

The Midshires Way to Duffield

Map 14

1. Pass back of farm buildings, follow farm track to a lane. Turn right at the lane Follow Midshires Way sign on right bearing right to a stream on a walled footbridge. Bear left through a gate and down to Watergate Farm. Follow way-marked field paths across several fields; at Home Farm the path meets a minor road; turn right and follow the road.

2. Enter Alderwasley Hall grounds. The field path goes through a farm gate. At the cairn go right and continue on track. At Information cairn again go right where the track forks. Come to a road and go straight across it; leaving Shining Cliff woods.

3. Continue on the road for a short while: at a fork in the road bear slightly right and then follow the path in almost a straight line for close on three miles. You will see the Derwent River now some distance away on your left, and traffic on the A6 alongside the river. You will pass through stiles and past farms and the shape of Belper on your left begins to unfold.

4. You reach the Ashbourne Rd at Blackbrook; (If you wish to stay overnight, you can walk into Belper. The road crosses the Derwent by a bridge and you find yourself in the shopping area of Belper) If continuing, turn right along the road for a short distance & past the Post Office. Turn off the road at a signpost on your left, by a ford and over a footbridge.

5. Follow this footpath, with Lumb Brook on your right-hand side. At a junction of footpaths at Farnah Green turn left on a path to Farnah Green Rd. Turn right on the road; then left; then right – to join the long North Lane which runs along the Chevin, a high ridge that has been a roadway of Celts and then Romans for more than two thousand years. But, as you stride along it ecstatically, on a bright sunlit day in spring, with the wildflowers opening all around you on right and left, know that you are now turning your back on some of the most beautiful countryside in Britain. You are saying goodbye to the lonely moors of the high Pennines, the gritstone of Kinder, the bright green of the grass on the white limestone of the Peak District, on the deep valleys where the Industrial Revolution began, and the hidden streams and waterfalls unseen from cars, planes or trains but feasted on by the walkers of the north-west.

6. You are passing over a golf course down to Duffield and over the River Derwent, into a wizened and tortured strip of land which fights for its survival as it threatens to be crushed between the monstrous greed of two opposing urban sprawls: one emanating from Derby which once gave birth to Rolls Royce, and the other, Nottingham, which gave birth to Robin Hood. And when you have crossed the Derwent you will enter a prelude to this, in a short but pleasant interlude of woodland and upland, through countryside, which once boasted a famous abbey and an ancient hermitage; but then the way will wriggle and twist and squirm its way towards Kegworth and the rolling wolds of Lincolnshire.

Midshire Way to Duffield

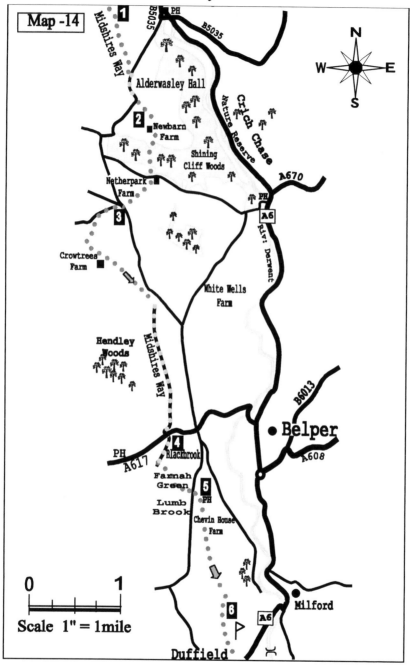

The Midshires Way
Duffield to Dale Abbey

Map 15

1. Come into Duffield on Golf Lane, following around the back of the Golf Club house. Follow down to meet the A6 as it enters Duffield via a bridge over the river Derwent. Walk through Duffield on the sidewalk of the A6. When you reach the Post Office look for the Midshires Way sign: it crosses the grounds of the Hall and crosses the railway by a footbridge to reach an old packhorse trail; through Eaton Park Wood and Little Eaton.

2. Turning left up Alfreton Road and then right over the road-ways and rail by footbridge and into Horsley Carr, turn right at Horsley Carr over five stiles to Morley Lane.

3. Turn left at Moor Lane and right at Priory Cottage Cross, Morley Moor and into Stanley. This is delightful walking, across open country and along well-defined lanes. It was while eating a banana, sitting on the grass and trying to light a cigar by sunlight reflecting through a compass, that I met a family from Birkenhead who live at Stanley. I did light the cigar! They invited me in as I passed their house and gave me tea and sandwiches. It was a lovely incident on the Walsingham Way; it was full of precious events like that.

4. Just before reaching the outskirts of Stanley, the path crosses the main road and goes in the direction of Brook House Farm. Turn right and at a criss-cross of footpaths turn left.

5. At public house turn right over the fields to Dale Abbey, from Dunnshill to Columbine Farm and the Dale Hills.

Duffield to Dale Abbey (Midshires Way)

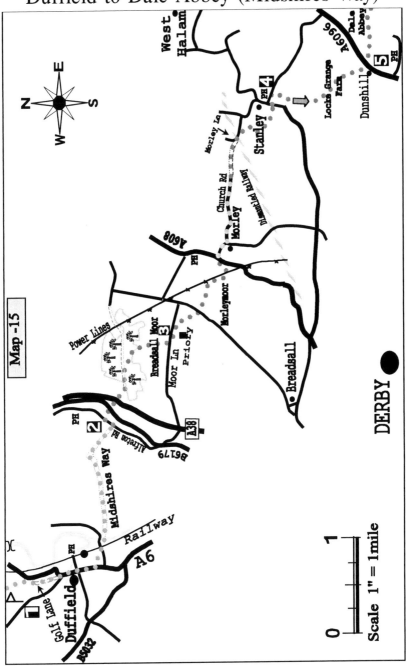

Map -15

The Midshires Way
Dale Abbey to Kegworth

Map 16

An up-to-date copy of O.S. Landranger 129 – Nottingham & Loughborough –
would be useful.

1. On the outside of the Abbey take the footpath through the hermit's wood and go south. At Hopwell Hall Farm and Constitution Hill turn east.

2. After a mile turn south again towards Risley.

3. Go through the Nature Reserve, past the Manor to the Blue Ball pub near the B5010 road.

4. Follow an underpass beneath the A52 and follow the Midshires Way across the fields, going south to Draycott.

5. Keep straight on, in a southerly direction, directly through Draycott and out the far side coming out with sewage works on your left-hand side. South east for some four miles until the path reaches a B Road. Turn right along it for a short distance and turn off for Great Milne.

6. Descend south to a pub on the Trent and Mersey Canal. The path runs alongside this all the way to the Sawley Marina passing under the M1.

7. Leave Sawley on a road leading to Warren Lane. Pass through a bridlegate into a culvert and follow telegraph poles across two fields. Come out into Ratcliffe Lane and turn left for half a mile. Then turn right and cross the A453 by a bridge, and you are now in Long Lane, which takes you to the outskirts of Kegworth.

174

Dale Abbey to Kegworth (Midshires Way)

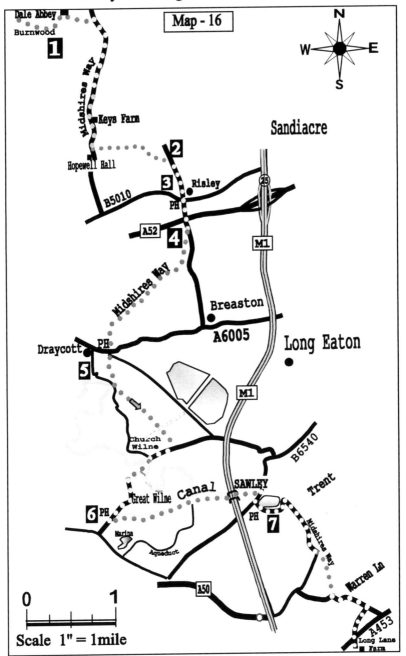

Map - 16

Dale Abbey
Burnwood

1

Midshires Way

Keys Farm

Sandiacre

2

Hopewell Hall

3 Risley

B5010

PH

A52

4

M1

Midshires Way

Breaston

A6005

Long Eaton

Draycott PH

5

M1

Church Wilne

B6540

Trent

Great Wilne Canal SAWLEY

6 PH

PH

7

Marina

Aqueduct

Midshires Way

Warren La

A50

A453

Long Lane Farm

0   1

Scale 1" = 1mile

The Midshires Way
Kegworth to Bunny

Map 17

1. Then turn right and cross the A453 by a bridge and you are now in Long Lane, which takes you to the outskirts of Kegworth.

2. Pass Carters' Lemonade Factory and Slack and Parr Engineers. Turn left at the first crossroads. Keep the sports ground on your right, and the allotments. Cross the Soar with the Anchor Inn on your right.

3. Cross the railway. Railway Inn on your left hand side, at the crossroads keep straight on. For some distance now you will be travelling on roads. Cannot be avoided. There are usually good wide grass verges.

4. Pass Scotland Farm and a row of modern houses on your left. You are now in Melton Lane. Come to the Star Inn (very good food!) on your left-hand side. Turn left at the crossroads by the pub, and then right into West Leake.

5. Go through the village and take a footpath leading past Fox Hill Farm on your right hand side At the T junction of bridleways turn right; pass the golf course on your left.

6. Enter Stocking Lane. Cross the railway turn down to the right, Gotham Road, and after a short distance turn left into Taft Leys Lane. Follow this past Hill Top Farm on your right up to the main road where you turn right. Gotham Lane.

7. Continue on until you meet the busy main road A60.

Kegworth to Bunny (Midshires Way)

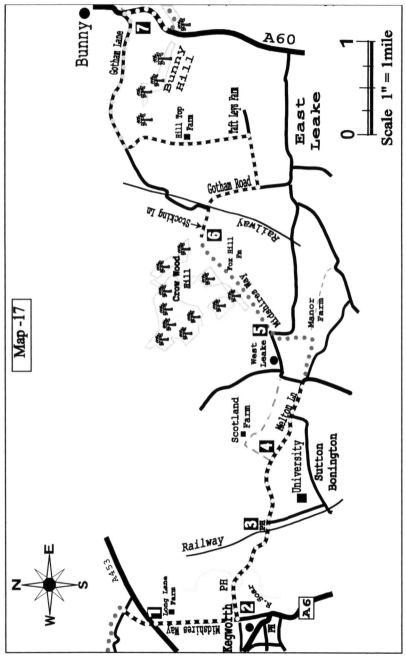

Map-17

Scale 1" = 1mile

178

The Midshires Way
Bunny to Upper Broughton

Map 18

1. You will see Bunny Old Wood on your left-hand side. Follow the track through the wood to an exit on the right-hand side. This is a footpath only. No cyclists and no horses. Unless it is too sloppy (as it can be), take it.

2. This footpath leads to Wysall. Go diagonally right across the field. Stile and ditchboards again after the next stile. If the weather is too bad – too sloppy – use the road and turn down right into Wysall.

3. There is a similar footpath crossing from Wysall to Willoughby-on-the-Wolds, This will involve twenty-three stiles and ditchboards. It will be marked for the Midshires Way; in hot dry weather it will be lovely. If the weather has been wet for weeks, forget it.

4. The road is only yards away; and has a broad verge. At Willoughby-on-the-Wolds take the road east. It is the road to Upper Broughton. It crosses the busy A46, by footbridge or underpass, at Broughton Lodge Hotel, when the Midshires Way passes Manor Farm.

5. It leaves the road to Upper Broughton and goes south. At this point we leave the Midshires Way.

Bunny to Upper Broughton (Midshires Way)

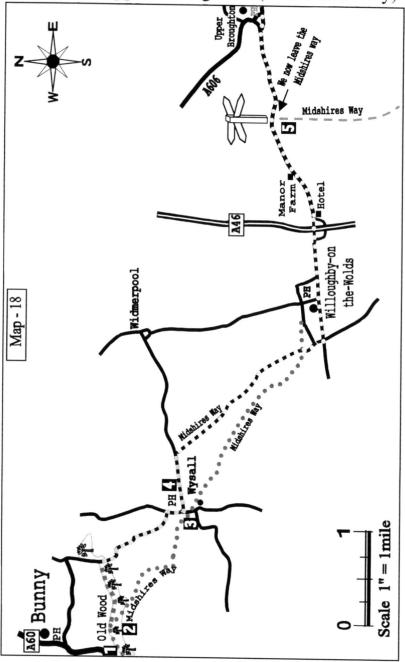

Map - 18

Scale 1" = 1mile

180

Mowbray Way
Upper Broughton to Chadwell

Map 19

1. At Upper Broughton you meet the A606, turn right (on a pavement) for some yards. Just before the road sign signifying end of 30 mph speed limit, you see a public footpath sign on the right (hidden by a bush) and a stile. Take this and climb over two or three other stiles, when you take the path to the left leading to Nether Broughton.

2. It comes out by a pub; cross the road to a further footpath sign which leads you through a children's playground. Cross the road and turn left and follow the houses round to the right. Then left opposite the red post box in the wall (the Post Office is not there now) and continue some yards down the road to a footpath sign on the right. This begins a well waymarked footpath to Holwell Mouth. Look for posts with yellow tops, crossing a stile and some fields: the farmers plough up the path but it is there. The ground rises up to Holwell Mouth where you meet the road again.

3. Turn left down this road to a junction. Turn sharp right at the junction and make for Holwell. These are busy roads. Kettleby and Waltham. Turn left at Nursery Lane to Holwell. Go through this lovely village. Over a cattle grid; rising ground. Then on the left a footpath sign diagonally across the grass to a stile. The path is very well marked. Done by the local Rotary organization. Despite thick mud and ploughed right up to the hedges. The path comes to a metal road at a

181

U-bend by the disused railway. There is a path opposite leading to Scalford, but it might be simpler to take the main road which is only for a short distance.

4. At Scalford make for the church and go round it at the U bend; continue down hill, past a Dairy Crest Creamery on the right. Swing right along the road over the stream. You now begin to follow Mowbray Way. It is well waymarked all the way to Buckminster. You come into Chadwell along Springfield Lane.

Upper Broughton to Chadwell

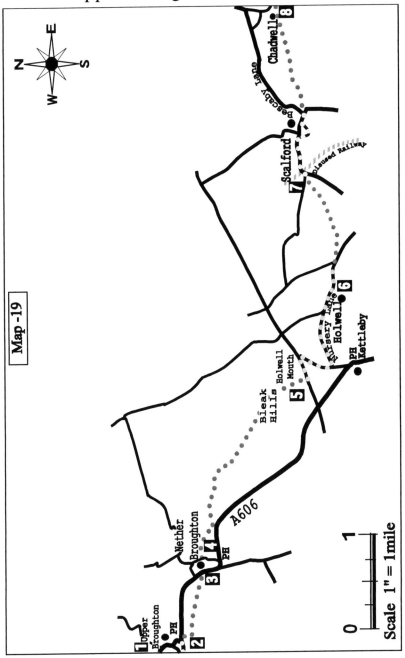

Map -19

Scale 1" = 1mile

Mowbray Way
Chadwell to Buckminster

Map 20

1. From Springfield Lane turn right: go along the road for some twenty yards and pick up the Mowbray Way sign. At the long field follow line of telegraph poles: diagonally right to corner of field, diagonally right again to corner of next field etc.

2. At Waltham on the Wolds. You approach by meeting the A607 road. Cross the road by a stile on opposite side; you go past a red brick bungalow. Go past the large sheds to a stile in the far corner of the field (diagonally right). Walk with hedge on your left to reach Stonesby Road.

3. Turn off this at Bescaby Lane and follow waymarks into Stonesby. Turn left along Main Street.

4. At a bend in the road see waymarker for Mowbray Way. This takes you to Sproxton.

5. Follow waymarkers from Sproxton to Buckminster. Here you leave the Mowbray Way. – Turn right at the Georgian Stables and then left along the Stainby Road. This is the Viking Way and you follow it for about half a mile.

Chadwell to Buckminster

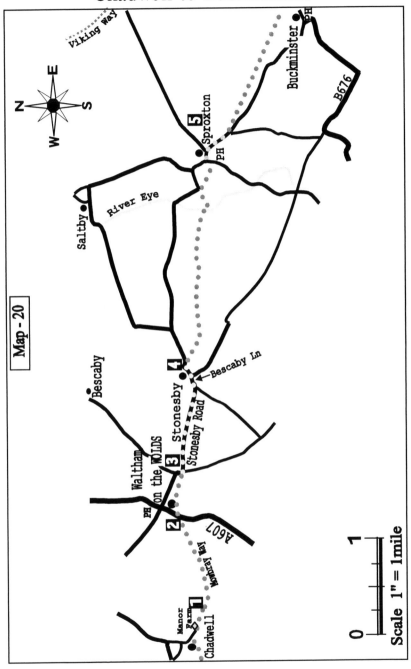

Map - 20

Scale 1" = 1mile

The Viking Way
Buckminster to South Witham
on to Castle Bytham

Map 21

1. Go down The Drift, also known as the Viking Way, for half a mile heading south, good green verges on side of road. At the crossroads go straight ahead, still going south.

2. Turn left at Moor Lane. After 1½ miles you pass some council houses and it becomes an extensive estate.

3. Turn right when Moor Lane reaches a major road, down past a small cemetery and go into the village of South Witham, down Church Street, past the Angel Inn and the church on the left-hand side. Path through the village end at the Blue Cow.

4. From here there are two paths to Castle Bytham, one follows a footpath down to Green Lane. A broad track, which leads to the A1. The problem is, it involves crossing the A1, which can be suicidal.

5. Hence it is better to turn left on the main road to Castle Bytham, the Blue Cow and Broadgate Road, and past Manor Farm. This has wide verges and it passes under the A1. After the underpass it shortly turns sharp right and skirts Morkery Woods.

6. There are two permissive entries to the wood. Take the second one, which has a car park attached and is the beginning of a woodland track, named Stone Drive.

186

7. This leads through the wood and along a farm track to a farm attached to a prison.

8. At the end of the track there is a junction of footpaths. Take the left one; it goes along a bank raised above a ploughed field between two hills (low). Follow the waymarks over the disused railway to the outskirts of Castle Bytham.

Buckminster to Castle Bytham

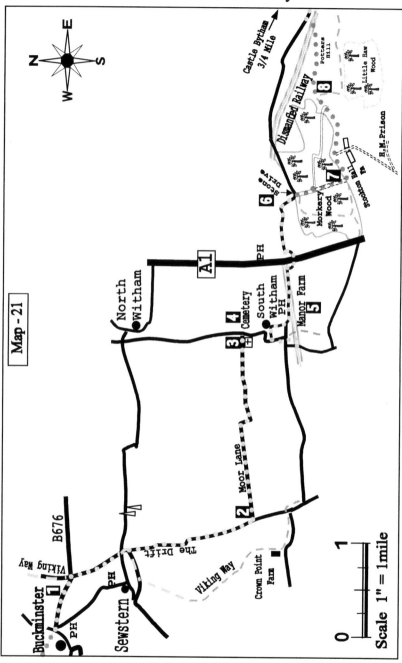

Castle Bytham to Witham-on-the-Hill

Map 22

1. Follow the waymarks over the disused railway to the outskirts of Castle Bytham.

2. From Little Bytham follow the road to Witham-on-the-Hill. A triangle of grass with a tall oak tree.

3. Take the road on the left, before reaching the telephone box. After some yards you see a public bridleway sign and also another roadway to the side of it. Best to take the public bridleway. It comes to a gate at the top of the hill and more sign posts.

4. Take path going right on the edge of the wood – a bit of a jungle, and churned up by horses. Come out into an open field and follow path downhill. Keep close to the hedge on your left as it winds down a long hill; at the bottom it meets a cart track going to a little hamlet.

5. At the T junction, turn right and walk to the Bourne Road. Cross the road and follow footpath signs to Northope and down to Thurlsby (ignore the last footpath sign on the right and go on to a lane). Journey into Thurlby and hope to get into the Youth Hostel.

Castle Bytham to Witham-on-the-Hill

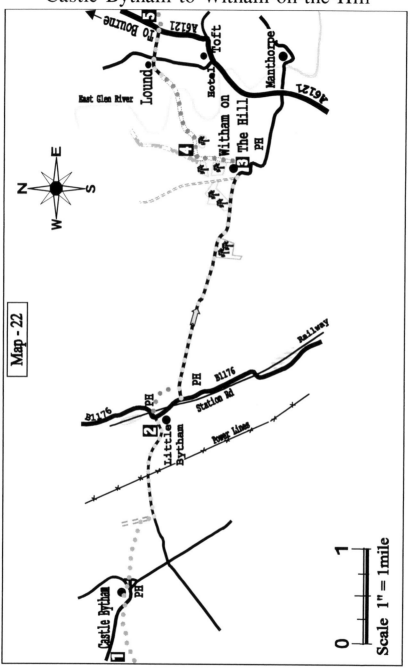

East Glen River

To Bourne

A6121

Hotel

Toft

Manthorpe

A6121

Lound

Witham on

The Hill

PH

Map - 22

N E S W

Railway

PH

B1176

Station Rd

PH

PH

B1176

Little
Bytham

Power Lines

Castle Bytham

PH

1

2

3

4

5

Scale 1" = 1mile

0   1

The Macmillan Way
Thurlby and through the Fens

Map 23

The Macmillan Way is a fully waymarked 290 mile, coast-to-coast path from Boston to Abbotsbury in Dorset.

1. At the T junction, turn right and walk to the Bourne Road. Cross the road and follow footpath signs to Northope and down to Thurlsby (ignore the last footpath sign on the right and go onto a lane). Journey into Thurlby and hope to get into the Youth Hostel.

2. Leave Thurlby by the road leading to Obthorpe Lodge and then the footpath to Kate's Bridge.

3. Cross the A15 and almost directly opposite see the open space and the footpath (the Macmillan Way).

4. This leads to the footpath along the Fen: keep along it (leaving the Macmillan Way when it crosses the Fen).

191

Thurlby and through the Fens (Macmillan Way)

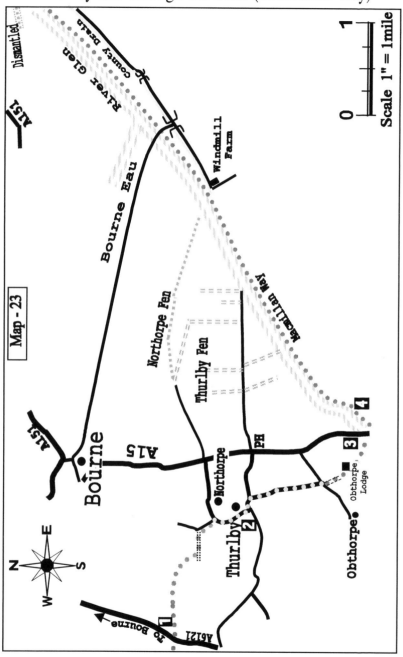

Map - 23

Scale 1" = 1mile

192

Through the Fens and into Spalding

~~~

Map 24

1. East to the A151 – into Spalding.

Through the Fens and into Spalding

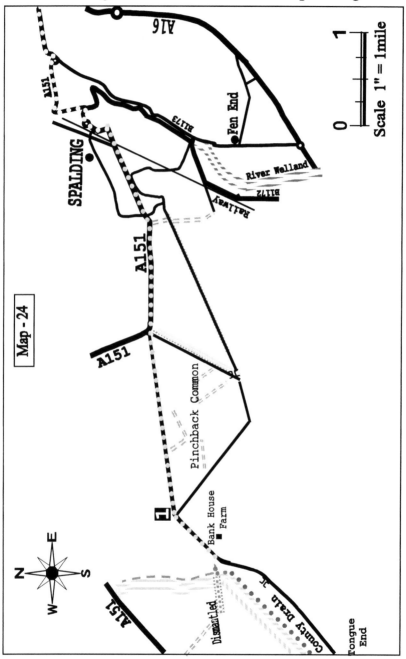

Map - 24

Scale 1" = 1mile

A16

A151

B1173

Fen End

SPALDING

River Welland

B1172

Railway

A151

A151

Pinchback Common

Bank House
Farm

Dismantled

County Drain

Tongue
End

194

Spalding to Holbeach

Map 25

1. There are no footpaths going east all the way to King's Lynn. It is necessary to use secondary roads. It is important to have with you Ordnance Survey map Landranger No. 151. With this you can plot a path using very minor roads.

2. But I can tell you for your comfort that I was on the A151 to Holbeach, and that there was a pavement all the way.

Spalding to Holbeach

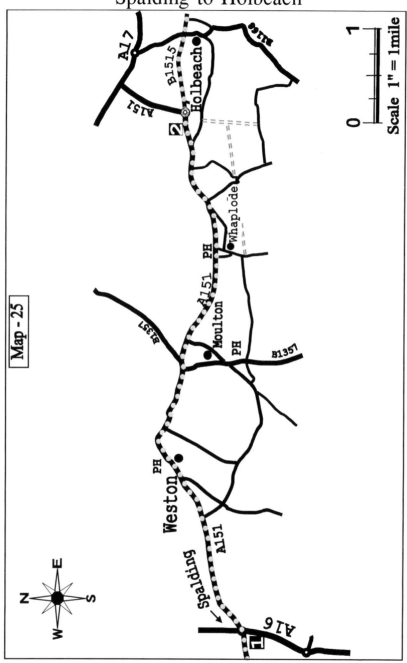

Map - 25

Scale 1" = 1mile

196

Holbeach to Little London

Map 26

1. At Fleet Hargate take the side roads to Gedney and there cross the horrendous A17.

2. Follow the road to Gedney Dyke / Chapelgate. Go to Chapelgate and then on to Little London.

Holbeach to Little London

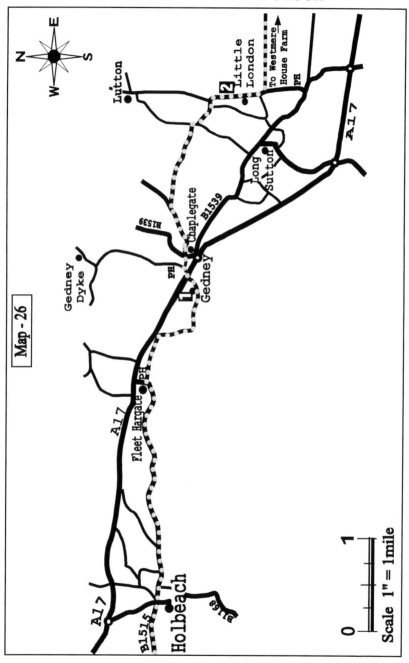

Map - 26

Scale 1" = 1mile

Little London to Terrington St Clement

Map 27

1. Continue south at the crossroads until you meet a road on your left going east: Westmere House farm.

2. Continue past the farm on the track to the T-junction and there turn right for Sutton Bridge

3. Cross the river at Sutton Bridge – immediately turn left on a roadway along the river.

4.Take the first road on the right and continue on this, until you turn right again to reach Walpole Cross Keys.

5. Take the road to Terrington St Clement (and thence to King's Lynn). This route takes you through some ancient towns which were the centre of the wool trade which made England rich in the middle ages. Hence the beautiful medieval churches and statues. But! If you value your life keep off the A17.

Little London to Terrington St Clement

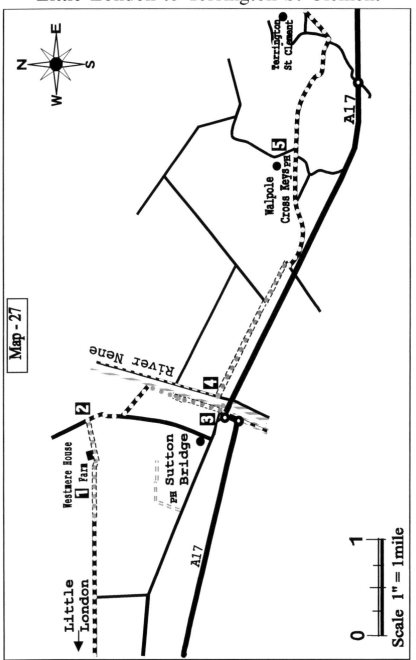

Terrington St Clement to King's Lynn

Map 28

1. Continue on the old road, passing Clenchwarten on your left, two miles on, the river Ouse comes into view

2. In the summer months an alternative is to use the ferry crossing at West Lynn which takes you to the centre of King's Lynn; this will save you over three miles of walking.

3. Cross the bridge over the Great Ouse, and follow the road as it turns left over the river and goes through the housing estate to South Lynn. Continue to the roundabout and take the A1048 to North End; thence to Gaywood and then north to South Wootton.

Terrington St Clement to King's Lynn

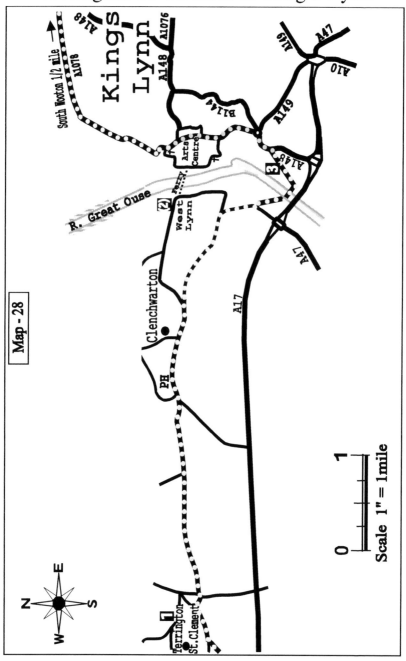

Map - 28

Scale 1" = 1mile

King's Lynn to Congham

Map 29

1. Keep on the A1048 as it skirts round the town, going first north then east to South Wootton.

2. At South Wootton follow the signs to the supermarket (Rainbow Supermarket). From the car park of the supermarket, turn right for some yards and take the road on left (Barsham Drive), and right again leading to a pathway running alongside a wood. It is a well-marked path and it goes east until it crosses the A149.

3. Keep on the Sandy Lane extension. Continue straight ahead; do not take the footpath on left or right. It passes sign for Spot Farm. Do not take the fork on the left; keep on main track. The road becomes a footpath with a field and wood on both left and right, almost a mile long.

4. Look for a Public Footpath sign on your left. It is down a slight incline and you can miss it: there are hedges screening a clear view, it leads across Roydon Common.

5. Cross a road and continue past Hall Farm. Take the farm road from Hall Farm: it crosses a minor road (phone box), and follow signpost to Congham, beautiful old village with medieval church and pub. Take left fork and continue east to the B1153. Turn left and walk some 300 yards to a Public Footpath and bridle path which leads to the Peddars Way.

King's Lynn to Congham

Map - 29

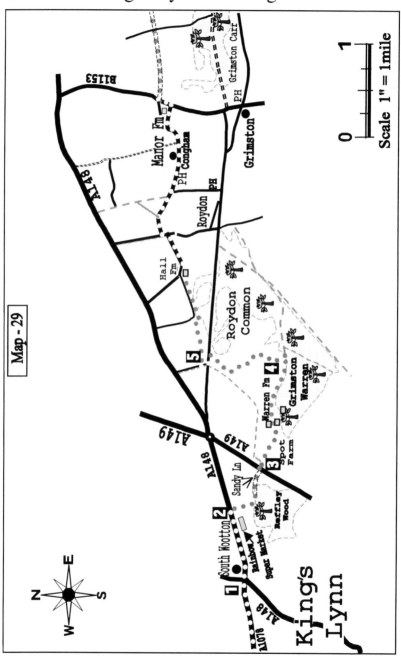

Scale 1" = 1mile

204

Peddars Way
Congham to Great Bircham

Map 30

The Peddars Way runs through Norfolk from south to north. Part of it is an ancient Roman Road. It is a straight line through the county. It is now a cycle track and bridle path as well as for walkers. It is hedged around most of the way, and provides an ideal method of moving up the county to a firm take-off spot to reach Walsingham. Thus from Congham to Great Bircham the way is on footpaths.

1. Go north when the bridle path reaches the Peddars Way.

2. Cross the A148. This can cause a little difficulty. It seems to break the continuity of the Peddars Way. It junctions with a minor road coming from the right and meets up with a stretch called Harpleys Dams. It continues straight north. Look around and you will find it.

3. Cross a minor road; cross the B1153. (If necessary you can take this B road directly into Great Bircham, but the desired method is to keep on the Peddars Way for a further mile, and turn right at a public footpath sign pointing you to the right. Over the fields on your right you should see a windmill). The footpath is about a mile beyond this.

4. You will see the acorn (designating a long-distance footpath) on the fingerpost. There is a large oak tree about twenty-five yards down on the left: follow the footpath to the road.

(4). There is an alternative to this. One mile before the foot-path described above the Peddars Way junctions with a minor road or lane. It forms a kind of crossroad, and I took a photo of that spot on my way to Walsingham in 1996. That minor road goes straight to Bircham Tofts and then on to the foot-paths to South Creake and it is an easier way.

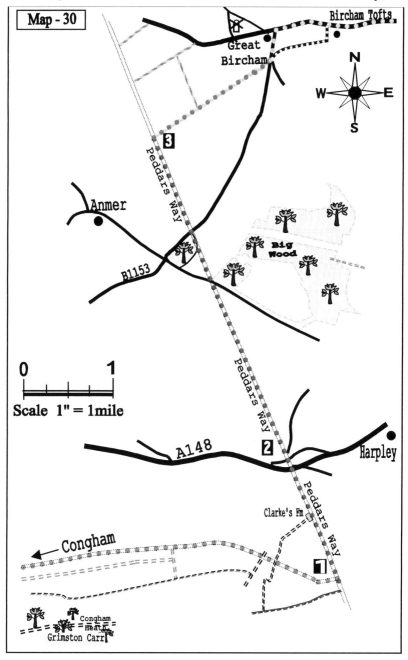

Map - 30

Bircham Tofts

Great
Bircham

3

N
W · E
S

Anmer

Peddars Way

B1153

Big
Wood

0   1

Scale 1" = 1mile

Peddars Way

A148   **2**   Harpley

Peddars Way

Clarke's Fm

Congham

1

Congham
Heath
Grimston Carr

Great Bircham to South Creake

Map 31

1. If you have taken the road to Great Bircham simply follow the B1155. Turn east until you meet the minor road coming from Bircham Tofts. The A road swings up north. The minor road goes east, signposted to Syderstone.

2. If you have gone to Bircham Tofts turn left; pass the church and the junction of Syderstone Road and the B1155; turn east on the Syderstone Road: about two miles along it, it skirts a wood first on the left and then it enters it. As it leaves the wood for open country you will see a path on the left which crosses the B1451 and continues on to Barmer.

3. It becomes a path alongside a wall then joins a minor road leading into South Creake.

Great Bircham to South Creake

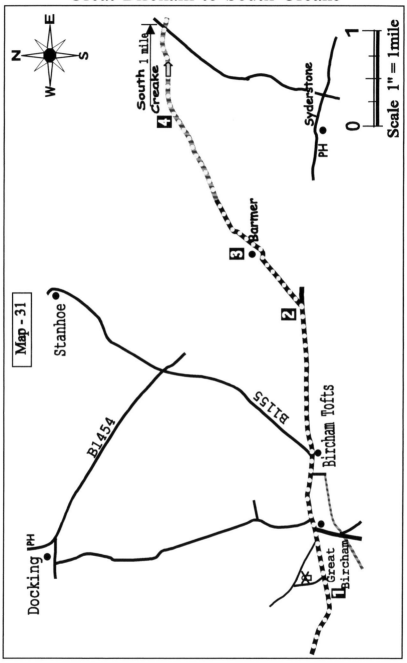

South Creake to Walsingham

Map 32

1. At South Creake you will find a circle of roads with a road running through the circle. Make for the public house. It is on the B1355. Follow it south-east on the B road.

2. Pass the entrance to Compton Hall and soon after take a minor road on the left. Keep on it all the way,

3. Passing Waterden Farm on your left and going through North Barsham Farm to the tiny hamlet of North Barsham, there you will see the signpost to the Slipper Chapel.

South Creake to Walsingham

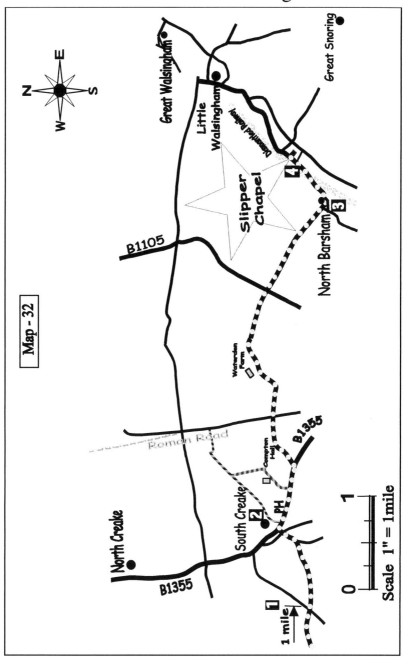

Map - 32

Scale 1" = 1mile

211